WICKED
CHARLOTTE

WICKED
CHARLOTTE

THE SORDID SIDE
OF THE QUEEN CITY

STEPHANIE BURT WILLIAMS

THE
History
PRESS

Published by The History Press
Charleston, SC 29403
www.historypress.net

Cover Image: 1926 vintage postcard of North Tryon Street at night. *Courtesy of the Robinson-Spangler Carolina Room of the Public Library of Charlotte and Mecklenburg County.*

First published 2006
Second printing 2013

Manufactured in the United States

ISBN 978.1.59629.160.7

Library of Congress CIP data applied for.

Notice: The information in this book is true and complete to the best of our knowledge. It is offered without guarantee on the part of the author or The History Press. The author and The History Press disclaim all liability in connection with the use of this book.

For Dad, whose love of the past created another
"history buff" in the family.

CONTENTS

CONTENTS

A classic Charlotte street scene from its trolley era. Charlotte was built on business and liked new technology, such as the electric streetcar. *Courtesy of the Robinson-Spangler Carolina Room of the Public Library of Charlotte and Mecklenburg County.*

ACKNOWLEDGEMENTS

Thanks first to the Robinson-Spangler Carolina Room of the Public Library of Charlotte and Mecklenburg County, whose wonderful files gave me a great start and especially to Sheila Bumgarner for her help in gathering many of the photographs. Thanks most of all to Bob for his encouragement and for being a part of my every day.

INTRODUCTION

Charlotte is not necessarily considered a "wicked" place. Evil is not evident in the shiny buildings and tree-lined streets of the Queen City. It's not a New Orleans, a Charleston or a Memphis that drip with folk tales around every corner, or make their tourism dollars with history tours and carriage rides. But despite the fact that it is one of the fastest-growing cities in the nation and it is forward thinking in much of its architecture and policies, it has a past, and a long one at that.

Charlotte was an established crossroads town by the time of the American Revolution, and the fields of Mecklenburg County surrounding it were filled with farms and plantations. It was a place with people and history, and with that history came the good and the bad. It was a rough-and-tumble place at a trading crossroads, built on commerce instead of culture from its very beginnings. Many of the same ills that affected the American South as a whole did have a place in Charlotte, both during the antebellum period and after it.

But it is its history post-1950 that really started to distinguish it from other cities. Very quickly, it went from a large Southern town to a bustling Southern city, new buildings replacing old structures in the center city as the business of banking became the business of Charlotte. Transfers and transplants started pouring in from other parts of the country, and for a while, Charlotte did not know who

The southwest corner of North College and East Fifth Streets in 1900. *Courtesy of the Robinson-Spangler Carolina Room of the Public Library of Charlotte and Mecklenburg County.*

it was, a little Atlanta or a big Birmingham. But it is neither. It is something else—a mixture of old and new that at last is admitting its place in the past as well as the future. It is the New South City, but it has roots in the Old South and the past in general, not all pretty and not all proud.

Charlotte is my hometown and the birthplace of my ancestors. There are wonderful people in Charlotte who will refill your tea glass without a word, smile at you in line at the bank and offer you a seat in the pew beside them at church. These are my friends, my past coworkers and my family. These are my people. But this book is not about those people.

In the history of any place, there are those who are not interested in living peacefully side by side with one another. For whatever reason, be it greed, jealously, desire of power or just plain spite, they make

Williams Cicero Warner Sr. (on left), my great-grandfather, and unidentified friend, circa 1910. *Courtesy of W.S. Burt Family Collection.*

decisions that lead them down a path decidedly different from those Charlotteans I call neighbors. This book is about them and the deeds they did.

Although we do not want to admit it, they are part of Charlotte history too, and the filling in of their stories will make us better appreciate our own, not just for what we have, but for the things from which we have turned away.

GREED IS THE COLOR OF GOLD

GOLD MINING IN CHARLOTTE'S EARLY HISTORY

Some might say that Charlotte has always been ruled by money. It is all about what you have, what you spend and how you show it off. New neighborhoods of houses decorated like wedding cakes show off new money in areas all over the Charlotte region, from the new money glittering all along the banks of the fake Lake Norman to the neo-traditional neighborhoods of southwestern Mecklenburg County.

Old money rules the center city, and it's not about how much you have—that's a given—but who your mother was and where you father attended college, practices law or other such pedigrees. And if you do not have old money, there's no way to get it, although Charlotte is a little more forgiving than a lot of traditional Southern cities. New money can become old money in as little as two generations. That is how we are, rewarding the new money for staying around.

Our tallest buildings are built by, named after and home to many of the country's largest banks. After all, according to the Charlotte Chamber, more banking resources are headquartered in Charlotte than in all but one U.S. city. This town is focused on money—the ways to make it, manage it, what to buy with it. How did this sleepy little town at a crossroads in the North Carolina Piedmont become such a powerhouse of banking, commerce and general commercialism? Well, we came by it naturally. There was gold scattered all through the rolling hills of the Piedmont that surrounded those crossroads.

That's right—this sleepy little crossroad held a secret of the most primal greed just below the surface. Creeks wound all throughout the countryside, and as they cut gently into the land they revealed shallow veins of gold. Gold is a shaper of nations. It drove Cortez deep into the Aztec jungles. It fueled some of the greatest wars in antiquity. And it definitely shaped the United States.

Gold, or the quest for it, brought many of the first settlers of the Southern United States to this land, and many accounts have the first pilgrims needing that first Thanksgiving meal from the Native Americans because they had squandered the harvest season carousing the Backcountry, looking for gold. But the first gold rush, that feverish migration of peoples with "get rich quick" shining in their eyes, was to begin in the Charlotte region.

By 1750, Charlotte was already a center of commerce, having established trade routes to the important port of Charleston, South Carolina. But it wasn't until after the Revolutionary War that Charlotte hit upon what was to become its present legacy: riches, and especially that all-important type of wealth, the "instant" wealth.

THE FIRST GOLD RUSH IN AMERICA

In 1799, on or very near the line of Cabarrus County (northeast of Charlotte) and Mecklenburg County, a young boy in a German-speaking farming community decided to play hooky from church. What he came back with (instead of finding spiritual riches in the ritual and Bible verses read aloud in the Sunday service) were more earthly riches than someone of his station was ever supposed to see.

One Sunday, supposedly in the spring, Conrad Reed chose to go fishing with several siblings in Little Meadow Creek on his father's property. It was one of the first warm days, and the boy probably had spring fever and didn't want to attend the stern German church with his parents. As he sat busily fishing with his siblings on the creek side, something glinting in the water caught his eye. In fact he described it as "a yellow substance shining in the water." Conrad was a curious boy, so, as many typical twelve-year-old boys would do, he waded in to retrieve the substance, discovered it was some sort of metal and decided to tote it home with him. The wedge-shaped rock was about

GREED IS THE COLOR OF GOLD

Little Meadow Creek looks much as it did that day in 1799 when Conrad Reed found the first nugget of Carolina gold. *Courtesy of North Carolina Historic Sites, Division of Archives and History.*

the size of a small smoothing iron or flatiron. Its weight was later said to be approximately seventeen pounds.

John Reed, a farmer, was Conrad's father. He was an illiterate Hessian mercenary from Germany — an illegal immigrant — who had deserted the British army in Savannah and made his way to backwoods North Carolina (and rural Mecklenburg County was definitely backwoods in the late 1700s), where he settled near Meadow Creek in Mecklenburg County.

In addition to being a deserter, Reed also had another dubious fact to add to his pedigree for wealth. Reed's father and mother did public penance in the church at Raboldshausen, Germany, a few months before his birth. His gravestone gives his birth date as January 1757, but church records indicate he was born on April 14, 1759. Did he want to hide his embarrassing past in his new home?

Most of the people in Mecklenburg County dwelt on modest family-run farms in rural areas, where they raised small grain crops such as corn and wheat. Therefore, if it were not for the seventeen-pound nugget, the names of John and Conrad Reed would have remained lost in history, another quiet rural existence, which was the norm in North Carolina during this period. But of course, there was that nugget.

After Conrad showed the yellow rock to his father, John Reed, unable to identify it, set the heavy rock aside as a doorstop and continued life as usual. For some time this valuable doorstop served unnoticed in its utilitarian role. In fact, this family walked past that rock every day, passing by more riches than they could even imagine, just sitting on the rough farmhouse floor. On only a single recorded occasion during the next three years did Reed pay any particular attention to it. At some point he took the hunk of ore to William Atkinson, supposedly a silversmith in nearby Concord, for identification. The silversmith was unable to recognize raw gold and could not identify the rock.

But, fortunately, that was not the end of the story for the illiterate German immigrant. Although he was uneducated, he knew the rock was unusual, and in 1802 found a person who recognized the raw gold at once. Dr. Richard Knapp, in his book *Golden Promise in the Piedmont: The Story of John Reed's Mine*, explains in detail what happened next:

> *A jeweler in Fayetteville, whom Reed visited on an annual marketing trip to that town, told Reed that the metal was gold and asked that the nugget be left for fluxing; when Reed returned, the artisan showed him a bar of gold six to eight inches long. It may be difficult to believe that Reed had no conception of gold as a precious item, but when the craftsman offered to buy the nugget, Reed asked what he felt to be a "big price" of $3.50. The merchant, whose name is now unknown, gladly paid him and received roughly $3,600 worth of gold.*

So the deadly sin of greed wrapped its tendrils around another's heart, and this jeweler most assuredly was proud of the great "deal" he had transacted with the lowly farmer. But his sin soon came to haunt him. Knapp goes on to say that it was not long before Reed discovered the egregious error and "recovered about a thousand dollars from the jeweler."

How did the Fayetteville jeweler suddenly have a change of heart? "Recovery" probably had something to do with force, especially since force was the language of choice for a Hessian mercenary who had been hired by the British army, then deserted into the depths of the newly forming United States of America. History does not provide the details, but Reed soon started systematically searching for gold on his property. He was not going to have to search long.

REED EXPANDS HIS BUSINESS

Reed used family labor, a common practice, to search for gold on his property, primarily in the summer. Farming did not require much labor at this time of year compared to other seasons of the farmer's year. Also, Little Meadow Creek dried to a trickle during the summer months. In 1803, perhaps uneasy with his changed status or perhaps uneasy with dividing his time among the occupation of farming and gold prospecting, he expanded his operation by taking three friends of relative substance—his brother-in-law Frederick Kiser, Reverend Love and wealthy landowner Martin Phifer Jr.—into partnership.

The Reverend James Love had been a part of this mining story from the beginning. He was possibly the one who "helped" Reed come to his senses and demand more money from the Fayetteville jeweler, and from that point forward the Reverend becomes intertwined in the story of the first gold rush in America.

Love was a slave-owning man, and he and Reed decided to employ two of his slaves in the first real mining season at Little Meadow Creek. It was common for ministers to have professions in addition to that of spreading the gospel, and Love most certainly did some farming in addition to being a Baptist minister.

In 1804, one of his slaves, Peter, found the biggest gold nugget ever discovered at Reed Gold Mine. The find occurred in the first real mining season on Reed's land. The nugget weighed twenty-eight pounds and was worth $131,264 in today's currency.

In later years, George Barnhardt, John Reed's son-in-law (two of John Reed's children married Love's children), told a story about the day when the nugget was found. Barnhardt said that Love offered Peter the opportunity to pry a knob off the gold nugget with his fork as a reward for his good work. Love reportedly said that if Peter succeeded in prying the knob off the nugget, he could keep it. According to Barnhardt, Peter responded, "No, master. I don't want to do that. I might break my fork."

WICKED CHARLOTTE

The Greedy Gold Fever Intensifies

But a gold rush is not just about one mining operation. Gold mining became a major industry in many North Carolina counties, including Mecklenburg, Lincoln, Gaston and Cabarrus, all counties situated in the North Carolina Piedmont. Though early census figures show men were employed as farmers, a great number of these farmers also worked as gold miners. Gold mining at its peak employed more North Carolinians than any occupation other than farming from 1800 to the Civil War. Entire families and many slaves worked in the mines. This included mothers and fathers as well as children, who from the age of five or six years knew how to search for gold.

In 1830, a Charlotte newspaper was begun called the *Miners and Farmers Journal*, because practically every farm in the North Carolina Piedmont had a gold mine on it or at least a prospect. The newspaper had many ads to sell mines that were deposit or placer mines near streams. Because most of the miners were uneducated farmers, the mining methods were primitive, and many speculate that because of that, only a fraction of the potential gold wealth was removed from the rolling hills of the Piedmont.

Historian Joyce Handsel documents the rise of North Carolina's gold fever:

> *From 1804 to 1828, all domestic gold coined by the United States Mint came from North Carolina. During that time thousands of foreign immigrants poured into the Piedmont area. North Carolina was known as the "Golden State." A small boost to gold mining did occur when immigrant experienced miners from England and Ireland entered the state.*

But as the technological advances created a mining industry in the Charlotte region, the mines became a rough-and-tumble place to say the least.

A tombstone in Spencer Mountain Cemetery (located in Gaston County, west of Charlotte) documents the death of a Mr. D.J. Simpson on December 12, 1878. It bears the words, "Died from wound at Duffy's Mine."

Eminent Charlotte historian Dr. Dan Morrill noted that most miners in the Charlotte area were the type of individuals you usually imagine in towns on the mining frontier. Morrill recounts the typical character of gold mining in his book *Historic Charlotte*:

> *A correspondent for the New York Observer toured the North Carolina gold fields in 1831 and was appalled by what he saw. "I can hardly conceive of a more immoral community than exists around these mines," he exclaimed. "Drunkenness, gambling, fighting, lewdness, and every other vice exists* [sic.] *here to an unlawful extent." A reporter from Charleston, South Carolina expressed similar dismay, noting that "business is* [sic.] *neglected through the week, and even the churches deserted on the Sabbath, to search for the corrupting treasure!"*

Handsel recalls another malicious event surrounding the greed that mining brought to the Charlotte region:

> *In June of 1926, on her 88th birthday celebration, Mrs. Lanira Robinson, daughter of Mr. William Benjamin Smith, who was a son of Peter Smith, was reminiscing about the mining of gold in the days past. She said her father had no mining experience and had employed his brother-in-law, Mr. William Richards, and Mr. Richards' two brothers, who were from England, to do his mining. A hidden rich vein of ore had been discovered that far exceeded any these miners had seen in England.*
>
> *Mrs. Robinson said that Mr. Richards offered her father $6,000 for the 45 acre tract of land and Mr. Smith was about to accept the offer when his daughter persuaded him to decline. Afterwards Mr. Smith learned of the rich vein of gold.*
>
> *In an act of revenge, the story goes, Mr. Richards destroyed the shafts and refused to work the mines, leaving them to the elements. As time went by the exact location of the mine shaft was concealed by growth of plants and trees. Years later the tract of land was sold at auction and bought by Dr. Howard Reedy who rented the property to Mr. Wade Rutledge.*

So greed gave way to spiteful revenge, in at least Richards's case. If he could not have the gold, he wanted no one to profit from it. In fact, the next generation at Reed Gold Mine experienced some of that same spite, as money breeds dissent.

Mines had sprung up by this time all over the Piedmont region. And these were not individual farmers looking for gold under cornstalks and cotton. These were serious mines employing foreign workers and slave labor. Large mines like St. Catherine's and the Rudisill Mine (both located in Charlotte, St. Catherine's in the area where the Bank of America stadium now stands and Rudisill on Summit Avenue) were putting pressure on the Reed Gold Mine to produce and remain profitable in a league that was no longer exclusive. Reed Gold Mine was still employing panners and rockers, and the profitable massive mines to the south in Charlotte were employing new techniques of shafts and tunnels.

After his original partners died, John Reed allowed his sons and sons-in-law to operate the mine, while giving Reed one-ninth of the profit. One day, John's son George could not get to the mine because his wife and son were ill. So George sent his sixteen-year-old son instead to work the mine. That day, a thirteen-pound nugget was discovered. George's partners refused to give him a share of the nugget. They insisted that his son was not capable of performing an adult's share of work.

Father John did not want his children divided, and the seventy-five-year-old man attempted to pay George off using his personal resources. But George would not have it, and was beyond forgiving his siblings. He took his brothers and brothers-in-law to court and the mine shut down for ten years because of the legal wrangle, which George eventually won (he recovered a sum of money that just about covered ten years of legal expenses).

For those who did not find gold on their property, some still decided to try and cash in on the gold rush that was gripping Charlotte and the surrounding country. They employed a technique called "salting" when it came time to sell their property, a devious and sneaky way to make the land seem full of promise. One source gave explicit advice for succeeding in such deception: "Melt up a silver dollar or a small gold piece…Divide them into small particles by throwing it into a basin of water while hot…Then scatter them about your spring, or in a branch where the road crosses it…Let some of your neighbors discover them by accident."

CRIMES ASSOCIATED WITH THE MINES

As is documented, the mines in and around Charlotte were always rough, often lawless. Some mining superintendents attempted to control the vice-ridden climate of their mines by forbidding strong drink. Still other mine owners did their best to attract or even sometimes employ preachers to come and speak the gospel to the mining men. Still, despite these measures, crime was abundant among the mines and miners.

Some crimes resulted from the instant wealth factor associated with the prospect and mining of gold, and these crimes were more often personal than public. Take for instance James Capps, an impoverished farmer off Beatties Ford Road, five miles north of Charlotte. One day he discovered gold on the struggling farm and soon became one of the richest men in the county. But poor Capps did not have the disposition for his sudden change in financial stature. Morrill recounts in *Historic Charlotte* that

> the Capps Mine became the "most productive gold mine in Mecklenburg County, and perhaps in the state," declared the *Western Carolinian*. Suddenly affluent, Capps began carrying portable scales with him wherever he went, so he could weigh the gold dust he needed to purchase whatever he wanted. Unfortunately, Capps used most of his precious ore to buy whiskey. He died from alcoholism in 1828. A newspaper reporter declared that "the BOTTLE, that too common resort of those whom affliction has cast down, or some freak of fortune has suddenly elevated to a condition for which nature had unsuited them, cut short the days of this miserably fortunate old man!"

So Capps could not handle his newfound fame. For others, it was simply being around an industry that by its very nature employed exploitations in many forms. And still for others, criminal acts seemed natural.

Although mining in Charlotte waned significantly after the Civil War, many mines were still operating. Reed Gold Mine was among them and in the 1890s became the site of an alleged gruesome murder.

Two brothers, William and Robert Gadd, worked at the mine, and one accused the other of murdering a woman and throwing her body down a mine shaft. Although arrests were made and an intense investigation commenced, the local authorities reported nothing that could substantiate the brother's accusations. Still rumors persist that there indeed was evidence to support the brothers' feud. Legend has it that a tooth, a watch and a lock of hair were found in the mine.

But ghost stories and rumors swirl around Reed Gold Mine, including accounts of an Elanor Mills, whose other-worldly voice could still be heard shrieking from her long-dead corpse. Her husband, in terror, allegedly threw her body down a shaft, where the voice still drifted up to his ears.

So it seems that mine shafts, at least the ones at Reed Gold Mine, were pretty handy for stowing bodies.

SLAVE LABOR IN THE MINES

Slaves were often sent to the mine as punishments. Historic Rosedale Plantation has records that indicate that a slave from that plantation was sent to the mines for three years, possibly as a punishment.

Slaves who worked at gold mines generally labored during the off-seasons. They had to do some of the most claustrophobic and dangerous work. Gold mine operators who were after quick profits sometimes made slaves dig directly into hillsides without giving them the opportunity or time to make sure the roof was secure. According to facts on the Reed Gold Mine web site, the earth, according to one historian, "often gave way and crushed the workers."

Some slaves, however, were able to use the mines, no matter the hellish work, to work harder and longer to purchase their freedom. Slave miners also earned money for doing "extra work" and made up to thirty dollars a month that way. Although the cultural view of slavery suggests that most slaves worked a specific job on a large plantation, in fact slave owners also trained skilled workers who could become very valuable on the open market. A blacksmith was valuable, as was one skilled in the mines, or even a slave skilled at the craft of smoking meat. These slaves would be hired out to others needing a particular expertise for a contracted amount of time, and sometimes the slaves would earn extra money in these contracts. But not always, and depending on the craft, not often.

Some slaves used Sundays and holidays to prospect on their own. Overseers did not trust slaves, and watched them carefully. The institution itself bred distrust between owners and slaves, and the North Carolina Piedmont held feelings that were no exception.

The mines in the Charlotte region were winding, numerous and dark, and many slaves used these attributes to attempt escape from the establishment of slavery. Reed Gold Mine documents one advertisement describing a slave named Reuben and his wife Jinney, who were thought to be hiding in or around Smart's Mine in Mecklenburg County. John K. Harrison of Mecklenburg asserted that his slave, missing in 1837, was "lurking about Reed's Gold Mine."

THE CHARLOTTE MINT

Charlotte became a clearinghouse for most of the gold that was mined throughout the region, and a need soon arose for the federal government to commission a mint in Charlotte. It opened under the direction of Superintendent John H. Wheeler on December 4, 1837. Morrill said that

> *the need for a branch mint in the North Carolina gold region arose because of the tendency of many private assayers and minters to produce counterfeit coins. A Congressional committee reported that a lot of "imperfect currency" was circulating in and around Charlotte and the other boomtowns of the Piedmont. The imposing new edifice, which cost $29,700 to build, operated until Confederate authorities took it over in May 1861.*

The Charlotte Mint was very productive. During its twenty-four-year history, it minted more than $5 million in gold coins. The mint made half-eagle coins, worth $5; quarter-eagle coins, worth $2.50; and $1 gold coins. When the Confederacy took over the mint in 1861, it was used as a headquarters and hospital. After the war, the building was no longer needed, and in 1933, a group of Charlotteans bought the structure for $950 and moved it rock by rock to its present location on Randolph Road. It currently houses the Mint Museum of Art, one of Charlotte's finest crown jewels.

ROBBERIES
HITTING CHARLOTTE
IN THE POCKETBOOK

COMMANDO GANG ROBS BELK'S

Downtown Charlotte was a bustling place in the 1960s. It was the center of commerce for the rapidly growing town, and at the center of it all was Belk's Department Store on Tryon Street. An institution in Charlotte since the turn of the century, the department store was the height of shopping pleasure in Charlotte with its quiet departments and modern elevators. And yes, it held a multi-tiered expanse of goods like any modern department store. Going "downtown" to shop was the place to go, and Belk's shopping bags were the bags to be carrying when you returned home.

The Belk family itself was, and is, as close as it comes to Charlotte royalty. By the 1960s, the second generation of the Belk family was managing an ever growing chain of department stores, and with their innovative technique of buying in bulk to reduce price (something so common today in our country of chain stores), they were only moving up.

Then came April 1967. It was spring in the Queen City, and although the city was bustling during the day, after the end of the business day, often the light posts would illuminate only the budding trees on the downtown streets instead of the bustling crowds.

People crowd the streets of downtown Charlotte, circa 1950. *Courtesy of the Robinson-Spangler Carolina Room of the Public Library of Charlotte and Mecklenburg County.*

ROBBERIES

Night watchman Onan Smith Sr., age sixty-four, was just beginning his shift on the Saturday evening when suddenly his quiet night turned into one of the most harrowing experiences of his life, as reported the next day by the *Charlotte Observer*:

> *Smith told police that he was walking on the first floor when three men suddenly appeared in front of him.*
>
> *"He said they came from out of nowhere," Porter* [the police detective on the case] *said.*
>
> *A fourth man slugged Smith from behind before he was able to recover from the surprise. Porter said that Smith probably was hit with a pistol barrel, cutting his head and stunning him. The men dragged Smith up a stairwell to the fourth floor and handcuffed him to the staircase railing.*

But these were not the smash and grab type of thieves. This group of men knew what they were doing and had obviously put some serious time into planning the operation. They used acetylene torches to cut into the large walk-in vault on the fourth floor of the store, and once inside that big vault they also cut into three smaller vaults. "They were deliberate, cool and positive in what they did. It was a well-cased job. They apparently knew every cubbyhole in the store," Porter said.

That must have been the case, for the men felt confident enough with their operation to spend five hours inside the store, ransacking the jewelry department in addition to taking all of Friday's and Saturday's cash receipts. The men apparently also knew the store's night watchman schedule because it was not until the next watchman arrived on the scene that the men packed up the almost $200,000 in cash, $13,000 in furs and some jewelry and headed out the same door they apparently entered earlier in the evening.

In order to carry out their robbery plan, Porter said one of the men must have hid in the store until closing and then after everything settled down, unlocked the door to let the other men in. But although they wanted Smith out of the way, the one thing that the men did not want was a murder on their hands:

> *While others were occupied with the safes, one of the men returned to the first floor, found some adhesive tape and gauze and bandaged the watchman's bleeding head.*

"He did such a good job of it that the nurse at the hospital later thought the bandages had been put on by the ambulance crew that brought him in," Porter said.

Smith said that the man who bandaged him told him, "If you want to live, keep your mouth shut."

Despite the robber's careful medical attention, he still put tape over Smith's mouth to keep him quiet, keeping him from alerting anyone that might come to his aid. Five hours later when Floyd Helms, the relief night watchman, and the store supervisor found him, Smith was in medical shock, still chained to the railing. He had managed to maneuver a watch out of his shirt pocket to check the time, but other than that, he had simply listened to the men moving about the store, looting and robbing, for an exhausting five hours. The handcuffs used on Smith had to be cut off him with a hacksaw, as they were not standard issue police handcuffs. Smith was taken to the hospital to be treated for the cut on his head and his shock. The police did attempt to get a statement from him later at the hospital, but he was not immediately useful as he was under heavy sedation.

Although the thieves probably had secured alternate transportation, they nevertheless stole Smith's car, which was found the next day in a parking lot at the Manger Motor Inn on North Tryon Street.

Captain Porter, the detective on the case, was sure that these men were not from the Charlotte area. Through the law enforcement pipelines, he had already heard of a gang robbing and looting up and down the East Coast, and he thought that the men that hit Belk's were part of the same gang. Why? Porter suspected the men used the ultra-modern technology of walkie-talkies to communicate with each other while executing the department store heist. Although Smith could not confirm the presence of walkie-talkies at the scene of the crime, both Porter and Smith acknowledged that the plan was well executed and that the men executing it had great communication with each other.

But walkie-talkies or not, Porter was nevertheless convinced that the "commando-like gang" that robbed the Belk's that Sunday evening had been from outside the Charlotte area. "'There's nobody around here with sense enough to pull a job like this,'" Porter was quoted as saying in the *Charlotte Observer* the next Monday.

THE LOOMIS FARGO THEFT

It was a scenario cooked up by two people in a pickup truck behind a Gaston County shooting range. "We will steal 17 million dollars, and with the help of your friend Steve, I will get a new identity and flee to Mexico. After the coast is clear, you'll join me and we will be lovers with millions of dollars."

What captured national attention is what the characters involved in the robbery did with their money—and how the FBI eventually apprehended them. Kelly Campbell and David Ghantt were those two people in the truck, and through Kelly's connections to a man named Steve Chambers, the team was able to steal $17 million from Loomis Fargo & Company in Charlotte.

Both Campbell and Ghantt worked at Loomis, and although they had never slept together, Ghantt had a major crush on Campbell and was ready to move with her to Mexico, leaving his wife and his credit-card-laden, small-time life in Gastonia.

The idea of stealing started out as a joke and then turned into a serious conversation and then into a plan. But when Ghantt was assigned a trainee to train doing pickups and deliveries, the couple decided it was time to "go for it."

Jeff Diamant, former reporter for the *Charlotte Observer*, covered the case from the beginning to end and wrote *Heist! The $17 Million Loomis Fargo Theft*. The book details how the actual crime took place on October 4, 1997. It was as simple as loading money into a van:

> *David and the trainee left the warehouse. In the parking lot, David sat in his pickup truck smoking a cigarette. When the trainee drove home, David waved. At about 6:40, he went back inside.*
>
> *The walk-in vault was a fortified gray room, more wide than long, with shelves, cabinets, desks, and multiple pushcarts stocked with shrink-wrapped cash. Vans could pull up inside the building and next to the vault, so outsiders couldn't see money being loaded. In preparation for his plan, David had backed an unmarked company Ford Econoline van near the vault entrance and opened its back door.*
>
> *His task was not easy. Though much of the money in the vault was already stacked on pushcarts when David began, other stacks*

were on shelves or the floor, and they were heavy. David was thin — six-foot-one, 165 pounds — and heaving the stacks onto the cart pushing the cart toward the vault door, and emptying its contents into the van was exhausting. Beads of sweat formed under his red hair.

He didn't stop with one cart…Stealing even a small amount, he reasoned, broke the bond of trust between him and his company as sure as stealing millions. And in the grand scheme of things, if he got caught, the prison sentence for stealing $20 million wouldn't be much worse than for stealing just $500,000 — maybe a few extra years behind bars.

Ghantt packed up the van, taking more than an hour to load all the money into the unmarked vehicle, and when the back gate of the complex was locked drove he out the front gate. Kelly was waiting for him outside the company with some other people in other cars, and they all caravanned down Suttle Avenue to Morehead Street and then to Freedom Drive and Interstate 85 after that. As quick as that, the group of unlikely robbers was outside of Charlotte and on to the next phase of their plan.

Ghantt fled to Mexico, waiting for Campbell to join him. And Steve Chambers, the lifelong crook who Campbell had brought into the group, had plans of his own. He brought more men into the group, including a nervous cousin, and after getting the cash back to his remote Lincoln County trailer, he added his wife Michele to the group, who, when she counted the cash, yelled, "I *love* this money!"

Steve and Michele never had any plans not to spend the money they helped steal. Steve felt sure that the authorities could never connect him to David Ghantt, so two days after the robbery the money started flowing out of that Lincoln County trailer. Whereas many robbers take their bounty and head for parts where they are not known, the Chambers couple wanted to show off their newfound wealth. They called it gambling money, and they spent it all under the noses of their friends. Their bad taste and unusual purchases caught the media's attention, and it was a classic case of "dumb crook news," a trail that cracked the case and sent its robbers to prison, and the money back to the bank.

On October 6, Michele deposited $9,500 in a NationsBank after asking the teller how much she could deposit without having to notify authorities. It was all in $20 bills

Steve and Michele had begun looking for luxury homes in their hometown of Cramer Mountain a few weeks before the heist. They moved from a trailer into a $635,000 home with seven thousand square feet and a curved staircase. At the closing, the couple showed up with $53,000 worth of money orders and $430,000 in cash in two black bags, all in $20 bills.

The house was decorated with a tiger-printed stair runner, a bust of Caesar on a pedestal, a tanning bed and a marble-walled walk-in shower, among other things. After the case broke, authorities also discovered a velvet Elvis painting, but the couple said that it had been a gag gift. The clown-faced lava lamp and the leather-padded headboard in the master bedroom apparently were not gags—they were décor.

For Christmas 1997, Steve bought Michele a $43,000 diamond ring.

All this time Ghantt was in Mexico, eating M&Ms, drinking tequila and reading comic books, waiting for Kelly to join him with the money. That was never going to happen because Chambers had another idea: kill Ghantt in Mexico and keep his share of the money. Kelly didn't want him killed but she didn't want to move there with him either, and, high on marijuana on Halloween night, she agreed to Steve's plan. And who would commit the murder? Mike McKinney, the man who'd sold his birth certificate and ID to Chambers for Ghantt's use in Mexico. McKinney would be killing his identity.

But all that never happened. There was just too much money floating around and too many people involved. The FBI started following the money trail and it was the group's phone conversations that eventually incriminated them. The robbers and accomplices, eight of them, were rounded up in February and March of 1998. It was an international investigation led by the FBI branch located in Charlotte, and it involved Interpol going to Mexico to extradite Ghantt. After all that waiting, he was glad to see them.

GANGSTER HEIST DEFINES CHARLOTTE'S "CRIME OF THE CENTURY"

What city comes to mind when one thinks of the term "gangster"? New York City? Chicago? Charlotte? The last is hardly likely, yet Charlotte played a pivotal role in the trial of a famous Chicago gangster for allegedly kidnapping Jake "the Barber" Factor.

WICKED CHARLOTTE

Roger Touhy, Chicago gangster extraordinaire, was awaiting trial in Chicago. The Touhy Gang hatched a plan to "raise some money," and one of the newest members of the Touhy Gang was chosen to go south to Charlotte for his part of the dough.

Mike Thomas, staff reporter for the *Illinois Police and Sheriff's News*, mentioned Touhy as among the foremost of Irish gangsters that controlled Chicago during the '30s, big enough to take on Capone himself:

> *Touhy, the blustery son of a cop, controlled gambling and liquor in Chicago's northwest suburbs. His take on slot machines alone is said to have been in excess of four grand a week. Capone long attempted to gain control of his territory, but Touhy, knowing what a gold mine he commanded, steadfastly refused to budge.*

Touhy's father was a Chicago police officer, but Touhy soon forgot his father's oath to uphold the law and earned the nickname "Terrible" Touhy. But when he was indicted for the kidnapping, he did not feel so terrible; he felt trapped, and he feared he was going to jail for a crime he swore he did not commit. On top of that, his mind was on money, being the Depression and all, and he wanted some quick cash to pay the lawyer for his trial.

In steps Basil "the Owl" Banghart.

Banghart had started working for Touhy only a few months earlier, but he had been in the criminal business for a number of years. Born in Michigan, he spent his life thieving and scamming, and then when caught, escaping from prison. Banghart was called "the Owl" for his exceptionally large eyes, and whether it was his eyes or not, the thief managed to escape numerous times from prisons, including a time in Atlanta when left alone for a few minutes.

In that instance, he called the police and told them that he was an FBI agent who had been overpowered by his prisoner, Basil Banghart. The police escorted him out of the building and when the truth was revealed, Banghart escaped in the confusion.

Even for Chicago gangsters, Banghart was among the toughest and most ruthless. In 1942, when *Time* magazine published a retrospective of Chicago's notorious criminals, Banghart was one of those earning that dubious distinction:

> *Slant-eyed Basil Banghart, 41, the Touhy mob's tommy-gunner, likewise was serving 99 years for the Factor job. Chicago detectives*

label him "a regular sharpie," tougher by far than Tough Touhy. Completely dedicated to crime and proud of his profession, Banghart is smart, energetic, fast-talking.

Whereas Touhy was a blustery blowhard (at five feet five inches, 139 pounds) who was quick to anger, Banghart was a con artist extraordinaire, labeled by prison sociologists as "sophisticated, well poised and astute." He completed one year of college, unlike many of his mobster "friends," so when it came time to travel down to the Southern city of Charlotte and "raise" some money for Touhy's trial, Banghart was the perfect man for the job. He could slip unawares into the sleepy city and come away with the cash, or so he thought.

November 15, 1933, dawned clear and bright, as Novembers often are in the Queen City. About three blocks from the railroad station downtown, a milkman was delivering milk and a mailman was delivering mail. It was a typical morning with typical happenings and typical outcomes. That is, until "the Owl" and his gang headed down the same street as that milkman and mailman. Years later, the *Charlotte Observer* ran a retrospective article detailing the 1933 morning's events. It was written by *Associated Press* staff writer Frankie Sharp:

> *The milkman cruised his white truck down the narrow dirt street, whistling a little tune into the crisp, sunny air. A big, dull-green mail truck lumbered toward him from the railroad station. Suddenly, a black car swooped from an alley and screeched between the two. It halted in a swirl of dust, blocking both trucks. Four men jumped out, one of them holding a submachine gun in his arm. The biggest holdup in Carolina history was underway—on a bright November morning here just 24 years ago next Friday. What did the young milkman do?*
>
> *"Well," said Harvey Morris, now a substantial businessman, "What would you do?" The shock and helpless outrage of long ago echoed in his voice. "I just sat there. That's what I did."*
>
> *The man with the submachine gun thrust its squat, ugly barrel in the stunned mail driver's face and grabbed his gun. Two other men snipped the lock on the truck's back panel with wire clippers, herded the mail clerk out with drawn guns and heaved the dun-colored mail sacks into the street. They carted them to the car and drove off.*

And so Banghart and his men, later identified as Ludwig "Dutch" Schmidt, Isaac Costner and Charles "Ice" Connors, rode away with more than $120,000 in $5 bills and other funds. Touhy had been in Charlotte a few days earlier and had aroused suspicion. Later many speculated that he'd been there trying to decide whether it was better to rob the mail truck or kidnap a Charlotte businessman and hold him for ransom. Obviously, they decided on the robbery, and from that moment on, had started planning the heist. But Frank Littlejohn was on the case, and although the robbery was well executed, Littlejohn was groundbreaking in how he approached detective work. And he was taking this robbery personally.

Sharp wrote:

> *"The dirt had hardly settled when we arrived," recalled Charlotte Police Chief Frank N. Littlejohn, who then was head of detectives.*
>
> *Littlejohn, a big, easy-walking man, calls himself just a country boy. But as one admirer put it: "There's a steel trap mind behind that corn pone manner."*

Of course, in cases like this, there is always a break. Littlejohn's break was an abandoned car, a black Plymouth to be exact, that was found abandoned on a rural road outside Charlotte. It was a car that had been documented as stolen from East Morehead Street two weeks earlier, and the owner said he'd had the battery checked right before it was stolen. What would this have to do with a robbery? Well, that's where the Littlejohn detective work came into play.

The head of detectives had noticed that the stolen car was almost new, and he knew that if it'd had a checkup, he could figure out a few things from that record. When he got the garage's record, the mileage noted showed that the car had only been driven nine miles since it was stolen. Since the Plymouth was found nearly nine miles from the scene of the crime, Littlejohn deduced that it had been stolen specifically for the heist—stolen and then hidden, actually pretty close to the location where the robbery took place. So suddenly, within twenty-four hours, Littlejohn had a specific area for his men to canvass.

Littlejohn recalled the next step:

> *A lady on 10th Street said two men had rented a room, but said they wouldn't take it without a garage. She said her neighbor had*

a garage and so they moved in. It was a dirt floor garage—you could see they'd driven that car in and never driven it out until the morning of the robbery.

The lady said there were two men, one with a pronounced limp. She said they walked west whenever they left the apartment.

The man with the limp was Dutch Schmidt, who had acquired that limp when he had been shot during another car robbery, that time for a Cadillac. Littlejohn traced the men to another hideout, where they had posed as an old retired preacher and his daughter and son-in-law. The "daughter" was later discovered to be Mae Blalock, Banghart's sweetheart at the time.

When the detective burst in through the door with his men, he found the radio blaring, a newspaper lying on the table with the story of Littlejohn's break of the base and three steaks still in the refrigerator. "The bird had flown in a hurry," Littlejohn recalled.

Littlejohn figured if they had left in that much of a hurry, there was probably some incriminating evidence in the apartment, so he gathered everything from the apartment. Police took the evidence to police headquarters and Littlejohn sorted even the garbage. It was there that he found the pieces of evidence that would define his career, that is, define him as a "birddog" of a police officer.

He found twenty-seven bits of paper, which, when pieced together, made up a receipt for $30.50 from a place in Chicago. This was important. This was big.

Littlejohn left that evening for Chicago and was there by the next morning. The boys had recovered some very readable fingerprints from some beer bottles found in the apartment, and Littlejohn needed to speak to the Chicago police to see if they could identify them. Of course, they could.

All four men were indicted, although "Ice" Connors never made it to trial. Sharp said that he "was found in a Chicago suburb, his body riddled with machine gun bullets and trussed with barbed wire, his dead fist clenched around a penny." Seems the mob got to him before justice could render its verdict.

Some of the money was recovered, but Banghart was sentenced to thirty-six years in federal district court in Asheville on May 15, 1934, for his part in the robbery. Then there was the Jake Factor business in Illinois, and he was convicted for his role in the kidnapping, receiving ninety-nine years.

John William Tuohy, who is a Washington-based researcher and has researched extensively on organized crime, documented the statement Banghart made when he sat on trial:

> When Banghart was called to the stand during the Factor kidnap trial, the prosecuting attorney, Wilbert Crowley asked: "What is your occupation, Mr. Banghart?"
>
> "Thief."
>
> The jury laughed but Crowley was confused. "What? I'm a thief. I steal…that's how I make my living."
>
> "What was the last place of your residence?"
>
> "601 McDonough Boulevard SE, Atlanta Georgia, but it wasn't permanent."
>
> Later in the day Crowley found out that 601 McDonough was the address for Atlanta Federal prison and called Banghart back to the witness stand to explain himself.
>
> "Why didn't you tell us," Crowley demanded, "that you were in prison?"
>
> "Four walls and iron bars," Banghart replied, "do not a prison make."
>
> Flustered, Crowley said, "So you escaped from prison, isn't that correct?"
>
> Banghart was indignant. "No. The warden says I escaped from prison."
>
> "And," Crowley asked, "What do you say?"
>
> "I say," replied Banghart, "that I left without permission."
>
> "The point is, Mr. Banghart, is that you are a fugitive, are you not?"
>
> "Yes I am. I am a fugitive."
>
> "From where, sir?"
>
> "Well hell son, from justice."
>
> The jury had a good laugh at the Owl's testimony but they found him guilty anyway. He was sentenced to 99 years for his role in the Factor kidnapping, plus 31 years for his part in the mail robberies.

On December 16, 1959, "Terrible Roger" Touhy and a retired sergeant of the Chicago Police Department were shot as they were ascending stairs in Chicago, Illinois. Touhy died of his wounds.

THE TASTE OF WHITE LIGHTNING

BOOTLEGGERS, SPEAKEASIES AND THE RISE OF NASCAR

BOOTLEGGING IN THE PIEDMONT

It is no secret that Wilkes County was one of the largest producers of illegal alcohol in the country. This has been touted in numerous history texts, and Wilkes County still has to fight against the "moonshine capital of the world" moniker. However, it was (and is) by far not the only place illegal liquor was produced in the state.

Mecklenburg County also was a producer of moonshine, and although not to the level of a place such as Wilkes County, it produced its share. Those familiar with Charlotte and its surrounding county can attest that it has always been a city in the midst of fields, rising up from farmland in the middle of the Carolina Piedmont. Practically, this means that it was pretty easy "to get out of town" on two-lane farm-to-market roads—and away from big city lights and big city activities. Little towns like Matthews, Huntersville, Newell and Mint Hill surrounded the big city, but where they have filled up with cul-de-sacs as bedroom communities today (some even swallowed in the city limits), they were once founded on the farming life—and that sometimes meant the supplemental income of moonshine that came along with it.

Moonshine, and the making of it, is in many ways a Southern tradition, especially in areas that were heavily settled by the Scotch-Irish. The Appalachian Mountains were filled with Scotch-Irish, and the North Carolina Piedmont had many from that area as well. Why is this heritage important? Because the Scotch-Irish people traditionally used the making of alcohol as a supplemental income and a way to avoid the heavy taxation of the British crown. If they made it from their own crops and then consumed the drink themselves or sold it to acquaintances, they could avoid what many felt was the persecution of taxation without representation. Sound familiar?

When asked why they willingly chose to break the law, most Appalachian moonshiners have mentioned that it was tradition and that the "gov'ment was trying to take a man's livelihood." There is a stubborn tradition of whiskey-making in the South that extends to this day, and although Charlotte's shiny buildings and chain restaurants might attempt to attest differently, ask the right people, and soon you will realize how white lightning is still seeping into the Queen City, fresh and as potent as it ever was, even though there has been liquor by the drink in Charlotte for years.

Moonshine went by many names of course, some of which were already mentioned here: white lightning, mountain dew, cool water and rotgut, just to name a few. The basics of making corn liquor are very simple and require simple ingredients that could be found every day on an average farm.

How to make moonshine:

Ingredients: sugar, corn meal, water, yeast and malt.

Mix all the ingredients in a large tub and then move it to a still to ferment. (This can be a simple jug or a complicated vat.) How quickly it ferments depends on the temperature, but after fermentation, heat the mash mixture to 173 degrees.

A vapor will form on the tubing leading from the still, usually coiled to fill an empty jug. The condensation is moonshine, and it is as easy as that. And as illegal.

Corn was a staple of the South. Nearly every farmer grew it, if not for sale, then for sustenance. Simply browse through a Southern cookbook and you will notice the amount of recipes that use corn meal or corn. We love our grits and we love our cornbread. Corn was easy, it was cheap and it was there. Turning the humble vegetable into high profit was the only sensible business move many of these sustenance farmers could see, and far from making them famous or above the law, it filled practical needs like money for shoes and feed for the horses. It was part of life, and it was always illegal.

Soon after the American Revolution, a whiskey tax became an economic issue in 1794. The "Whiskey Rebellion" broke out along the western frontier, present-day western Pennsylvania and eastern Ohio.

Revenue taxes were associated with the Union army during the War Between the States, and after the war when the Reconstructionist government decided to keep the taxes in place, the connection furthered the villainy of "the revenuer" in the eyes of the proud moonshining men.

After the Civil War, the Revenue Bureau of the Treasury Department was formed to officially collect lost taxes. During this period, the commissioner, Green Raum, actively transformed the collectors into a police agency that would seek out moonshiners on their properties. They were the federal government and therefore did not have to worry about crossing state lines.

In 1876, Zebulon Vance, a North Carolina senator, campaigned against revenue law. He said, "The time has come when an honest man can't take an honest drink without have a gang of revenue officers after him."

The modern history of "wets versus drys" is detailed by Blythe and Brockman in the 1961 book *Hornet's Nest: The Story of Charlotte and Mecklenburg County*:

> *The history of the liquor business in Charlotte differs only in detail from that in other North Carolina cities. In the early days, liquor was a staple article of merchandise in general stores. It was also available by the drink and in bottles at taverns. Later, saloons came into existence. These were forerunners of cocktail bars to be found elsewhere, but not in North Carolina, circa 1960.*
>
> *In 1900 there were fifteen saloons in Charlotte but here, as elsewhere, the prohibition sentiment was growing. The "morally stunted" as the "wets" came to be described, were finally defeated. In an election held July 5, 1904, voters were given an opportunity to vote for (a) absolute prohibition, (b) a city-owned dispensary.*

Total prohibition carried by a majority of 485. The effective date for the beginning of total prohibition was January 1, 1905.

The legal sale of alcoholic beverages was not resumed in Charlotte until September 25, 1947, when seven Alcoholic Beverage Control stores were opened. In an election held June 14, 1947, Mecklenburg voters gave their approval for the establishment of these stores by a vote of 16,377 to 12,830.

The period of history from 1904 until 1947 was the heyday of bootlegging in the North Carolina Piedmont, giving those hurt by the Great Depression a way to earn a good living, if not a legal one. Bootleggers were cooking, and Charlotte was drinking—and providing access to far reaching markets.

CHARLOTTE AS A DESTINATION FOR THE DRINK

Charlotte has always been a place for business. It was originally a crossroads for Native American trading, and many of its first settlers were

Business has always been a part of Charlotte, coming early to the crossroads. The Brown and Weddington Hardware Store, pictured here, was located on Trade Street between College and Tryon Street, right at the heart of the city. *Courtesy of the Robinson-Spangler Carolina Room of the Public Library of Charlotte and Mecklenburg County.*

merchants traveling from the Pennsylvania area down the Great Wagon Road. So when the railroad came to Charlotte in the mid-1880s, it was to spark an economic boom that Charlotte was ready to capitalize upon.

Just as the fact that Charlotte was surrounded by farmland made business good for bootlegging, it also made business good for farming. From Davidson in north Mecklenburg to Pineville in the south of the county, small farm-to-market roads stretched to the center of Charlotte, directly heading for the railroad station, where bales of cotton were loaded onto trains.

When the mills sprang up in the Piedmont, from Belmont to Albemarle to Charlotte to Kannapolis, those same rails would then transport the milled goods to the rest of the country, some even made from the cotton that had ridden those rails only a season earlier. Unlike many traditional cities that were settled near a body of water (a natural route for commerce), the rails served as Charlotte's lifeline of commerce.

Documentation of bootlegging, especially in Mecklenburg County, is somewhat difficult. Much attention and much press has been given to the mountain regions of Georgia, Tennessee and Charlotte's own state,

Cotton farmers gather in town, circa 1900. *Courtesy of the Robinson-Spangler Carolina Room of the Public Library of Charlotte and Mecklenburg County.*

therefore making difficult the pinpointing of exact numbers of how much liquor was flowing through Charlotte. However, as aforementioned, the textile industry west of Charlotte was heavily connected to the city by rail. *Mill News* documented Gaston County bootlegging in its publication on October 14, 1920. It is a given that much of that illegal hooch ended up in the big city:

> *Mr. George came to Cherryville twenty-seven years ago. At that time Gaston County was called a prohibition county; that is, there were no bar rooms allowed in the county, though whiskey could be sold at government distilleries. At that time there were forty government distilleries in the county, and possibly one hundred or more moonshine distilleries. He organized temperance societies while he was teaching school in Cherryville, and began the fight on whiskey business. He is now mayor of the town and still continuing this fight on blockading and drunkenness. During July, August and September the fines in his court amounted to over $1,100.00. Four blockade distilleries near the town have been broken up, and the mayor is determined to break up blind-tigers.*

And blind tigers bring us to the shadowy world of speakeasies.

SPEAKEASIES IN THE QUEEN CITY

Ever wonder why there are a good number of bars around the country named "Blind Tiger"? Well, the term "blind tiger" was a common code term for speakeasy. Patrons would pay to see the blind tiger, then get a drink "free." As to why it was a blind tiger? It was exotic, it was easy to remember and it could be compared to moonshine itself—bad hooch could blind a man, and if not, when it hit, it was like a tiger attacking its prey. No one ever said moonshine was easy-to-drink stuff. They just said it was effective.

Speakeasies in general were a place where alcohol was sold illegally and patrons had to "speak easy" to enter. This could be a secret pass phrase like "I want to see the blind tiger" or saying you were "here to see a friend." And Charlotte had been "speaking easy" long before the nation caught up with the "drys," as documented above.

THE TASTE OF WHITE LIGHTNING

The hidden bar was a new thing for Charlotte after 1904, and like the rest of the country, it changed social behavior forever. The realm of the saloon, which had been previously a place for males, was now no longer a bastion of male seclusion. Men began taking women on dates to speakeasies, the same men whose fathers would never have dreamed of inviting a "good" woman into a saloon. Women began to drink openly, and instead of the imbibing of alcohol being an accompaniment to the evening, it often became the main activity. Thus new social codes were established.

Speakeasies were also a great equalizer. Although there were of course different "grades" of speakeasies (from posh back rooms with private bands and comfortable booths to a shanty shack on a country road with mason jars for glasses and whatever entertainment happened to walk in the door), the crowds were united by their quest for illegal liquor.

Although the Jim Crow era was in full swing, speakeasies were often home to blacks and whites together, from Harlem in the North to New Orleans in the South. It seems that everyone decided at one point or another that they wanted a drink, and the construction worker might be sitting beside the milkman who was playing cards with a celebrity.

In 1931, the Charlotte Hornets were local celebrities. Not the NBA players of a much later era—the Charlotte Hornets were the Queen City's minor league baseball team, and they were often good and always fun to watch. None on the team was better than Frank Packard, who ignited the fans' hopes every time he took the plate. But there was a reason he never made the Majors. Baseball historians Bill Weiss and Marshall Wright document the reason:

> *The 1931 Hornets were paced at the plate by a brace of .300 hitters, none better than 23-year-old 5'10", 160-pound Frank Packard, third baseman-outfielder from Pittsburgh, PA. Packard won the Triple Crown by leading the league in hitting (.366), home runs (21) and RBI (123). In addition, he achieved league highs in runs (145), hits (185), total bases (313), triples (17) and slugging (.620). Charlotte fans dubbed him "What-A-Man" Packard in recognition of his exploits and that's how he was known in North Carolina the rest of his life. In 1932, Packard jumped all the way to Baltimore (International) where he had another fine season, batting .313 with 28 homers and 98 RBI.*

> *In "The Independent Carolina Baseball League," Hank Utley and Scott Verner said: "Charlotte Observer columnist Bob Quincy wrote (in 1982) that the one flaw keeping Packard from the major leagues was a lack of discipline. 'Socially, Packard would give blood before he'd turn down a party. He had a built-in radar to locate every speakeasy in town. Packard could discover soft lights, hard drink and pretty girls behind dusty doors or up broken elevator shafts at all hours of day and night.'"*

Packard subsequently never made the Major Leagues, instead staying in Charlotte and marrying a local girl who Weiss and Wright said Packard credited with

> *straightening out his life. He was an athletic director in the Navy during World War II and coached the Davidson College team for a year after the war. He was in the carpet business in Charlotte for many years. In 1982 he was named one of six charter members of the Charlotte Baseball Hall of Fame, along with former major league stars Harmon Killebrew, Tony Oliva and Hoyt Wilhelm.*

But during the 1930s, he was a fixture in Charlotte speakeasies, speakeasies that included Hotel Charlotte, many of the clubs in West Charlotte and countless back rooms of restaurants and pharmacies.

THE RISE OF NASCAR

NASCAR, once associated solely with rednecks and country boys, has recently moved uptown. With the addition of luxury boxes at many of the super speedways and the slicker images of the drivers themselves, NASCAR is no longer just the property of backwoods boys.

Despite its varied Southern history, NASCAR has long had an association specifically with the Queen City. In fact, NASCAR recently decided to build the NASCAR Hall of Fame in Charlotte after the city launched a massive publicity campaign for the museum. But why Charlotte?

Authors Marc Singer and Ryan Sumner attempted to explain the connection:

THE TASTE OF WHITE LIGHTNING

People from around the country are right to link Charlotte with racing—but they don't know how right they are. Historically, Charlotteans have taken a real pride in their cars, and their relationship with their vehicles has been deep and complex. Perhaps the history of the region itself has something to do with that. The Piedmont was historically poor, as was most of the South, but it was one of the first parts of the region to embrace the idea of the New South—a powerful view of social change, political progress, economic development and industry. Transportation—and the automobile in particular since it represented industrial progress— was a powerful symbol of the Piedmont's embrace of New South values. People needed good cars both for the work they did and to keep up with the rapidly expanding development of the region.

Naturally, when people who were proud of their cars met others with similar feelings, it was only a short step from there to racing. Automobiles allowed Charlotteans to combine their forward-looking mastery of technology with more elemental, fundamental passions.

Racecar drivers pose in front of the *Charlotte Observer* offices circa 1919. *Courtesy of the Robinson-Spangler Carolina Room of the Public Library of Charlotte and Mecklenburg County.*

WICKED CHARLOTTE

That's what auto racing is all about. Who's got the fastest car? Whose tractor can pull the heaviest load? Who has built the most reliable engine? Only one way to find out—and many did.

In fact, the first Southerner to even own an automobile was Charlottean Osmond Barringer. In 1900, he bought a pair of steam-driven Locomobiles shipped by boxcar from Bridgeport, Connecticut. He always had an interest in cars and their changing technology, and that interest would make him a pioneer in Charlotte's racing culture. Soon he drove an entire region into a love affair with their cars, cars that would take them far away from the mill houses and farm roads to the national media stage.

Add the above to the moonshine culture of bootlegging and you have that same pride mixed with men who can drive and know their own machines. You have the birth of NASCAR.

Many of the NASCAR greats have bootlegging backgrounds, but none so blatant as Junior Johnson, one of the legends of NASCAR. He has never hidden his bootlegging roots, and at many public appearances has even set up an old still and a favorite liquor-running vehicle beside his autograph table or in front of the building where he's signing copies of his biography.

In the introduction to *Junior Johnson: Brave in Life*, Cale Yarborough, who drove for Junior Johnson (when Johnson was an owner) from 1973 through 1980, credits liquor running as the root of all Johnson's success:

> *I know Junior's story well, and it is a fascinating one. His stories about his days as a whiskey hauler are riveting and often hilarious. Running moonshine groomed Junior for a racing career because he learned about cars and speed—and he learned those lessons well. When it came to racing, Junior was a no-nonsense competitor. He was bold and aggressive.*

Like many future stock car drivers, Junior Johnson came by his driving and bootlegging naturally. His father was in "the business." Born in Wilkes County, North Carolina (the self-professed moonshine capital of the world), Junior was driving liquor-running cars by the age of fourteen before he could legally hold a North Carolina's driver's license.

THE TASTE OF WHITE LIGHTNING

However, Robert Glenn Johnson, Junior's father, was not just a bootlegger as a sideline for extra money; he was a regular bootlegging mogul. Tom Higgins and Steve Waid wrote in *Junior Johnson* that

> *Although the number of moonshiners in Wilkes County couldn't easily be counted, Robert Glenn Johnson's operation was the area's biggest. By Junior's estimate, he built and ran as many as 1,000 stills in his lifetime…In 1935, federal agents raided the Johnson house and discovered a whopping 7,254 cases of moonshine. It was the single largest inland seizure of illegal whiskey ever made in America, the news wire services reported.*

Johnson would run moonshine for his father from eleven at night until six the next morning. Like most liquor-runners, he had regular rounds and would avoid delivering during the day, as it was too dangerous. Waid and Higgins describe that

> *The moonshine network started at some small, hidden still and stretched across the counties and cities in every direction. Junior delivered to small cities like Boone, Concord, Kannapolis, and Trap Hill. There were also bigger cities, such as High Point, Lexington, Salisbury, and Thomasville.*
>
> *The moonshine Junior delivered and sold might be sold twice again before finally reaching the end customer. The first buyer would make his profit by reselling it to someone else, who then might take it to another bigger city like Charlotte and sell it there.*

In order to do this type of delivery under the nose of the revenuers, one had to have reliable transportation. This is where the direct correlation to modern stock car racing becomes very clear: not only were the drivers part of the bootlegging business, but their modified stock cars also became the basis for an entire sport industry. It was not just Johnson's car that was modified; it was every bootlegger's who felt that they needed to go faster and go farther than the ones chasing them. Just in Wilkes County, Johnson estimated that there were at least seven hundred such whiskey runners. "'I'd see 'em all night long,' Junior remembers," wrote Waid and Higgins. "'I'd meet several cars, and I knew who was driving.'"

51

The point of the modern stock car and the whiskey running car are the same: they are supposed to look like standard body cars from the exterior, hiding a high-performance machine inside. The moonshiners didn't set out to build racecars—they set out to modify the machines they had to do the job asked of them.

Here are a few comparisons between whiskey-running cars and cars on the NASCAR circuits: for all that added weight, the moonshine cars needed heavy-duty suspensions. NASCAR's car suspensions are technically heavier and bigger than regular cars'. Motors were taken out and modified with high-performance camshafts, still a standard component of the stock car. There was no back seat in liquor-running cars, in order to run more whiskey per drive. There is no back seat in a stock car. The list could go on and on.

Junior competed in his first Grand National race on Labor Day 1953 at Darlington Raceway in South Carolina. The Grand National circuit was started by Bill France and would later become the NASCAR circuit. But being a legitimate racecar driver didn't stop Johnson from running moonshine. The racing money would not compare with what he could make running liquor—and it wouldn't for many years. Junior was arrested and convicted of moonshine in 1956 and served time in prison for his crime.

But as earlier stated, Johnson was by no means the only NASCAR star to get his start running moonshine: Fonty Flock, who won 153 races over nine years, got his start running moonshine. He started making deliveries as a teenager on his bicycle and then later with a car; Buck Baker, two-time Winston Cup Champion, used to run liquor on the back roads of North Carolina. He started racing full time when he was a bus driver in Charlotte; Wendell Scott, the first African American to compete in or win a Grand National Race, was a taxi driver and part-time liquor runner.

These men were just some of the men associated with moonshine and racing. There are countless bootlegging connections in the early history of NASCAR, from those who worked in the shops to the crews at the race track to the drivers themselves—moonshine built NASCAR, and that sport was born in the Carolina Piedmont.

SCOUNDRELS, CADS AND MISBEHAVING WOMEN

TEENAGE GIRL WITH ARSON ON HER MIND

"In April, 1952, a 13-year-old girl had church people sitting on pins and needles."

So read the *Charlotte Observer* in October of 1959 when it ran a retrospective story on crime in the Queen City. A thirteen-year-old girl was terrorizing the good churchgoing community of Charlotte. Charlotte, which at one time was flirting with the most churches per capita in the nation, was and is a churchgoing city. So it should be said that the girl "had *Charlotte* sitting on pins and needles."

Nevertheless, because she was a minor, her name was not revealed in the press. However, history has recorded the incidents that made her infamous, although she probably would not have thought of them as "infamous." She was just trying to use the phone after all, and when she could not, well, she had to admit she had a bit of a temper about it.

On April 16, 1952, the girl left her home and walked to Caldwell Memorial Presbyterian Church on Fifth Street. She asked a woman for permission to use the telephone, and the woman said that she would have to ask someone else. Instead of finding someone else to ask, the thirteen-year-old left angry. The woman and Caldwell

Memorial thought nothing else of it; that is, until that same night, when an American flag was burned in the basement of St. Martin's Episcopal Church, only a few blocks from Caldwell Memorial. The blaze was practically out of control when firefighters arrived, and the total damage to the church was around $21,000.

On April 19, fire struck Caldwell Memorial itself, causing $41,000 in damage. It was started in the cloakroom, and yes, authorities knew that these fires had been intentionally started. It was arson.

Local celebrity Chief of Police Frank Littlejohn was determined to catch the arsonist. He put policemen in every church in the eastern part of the city in hopes of catching the arsonist. What they picked up was a thirteen-year-old girl who had been denied the use of a church phone. But when they asked her about the fires, she talked. She confessed. It was she who had started all those fires in Charlotte's places of worship.

The *Charlotte Observer* reported what she revealed:

> *The girl said she set the churches on fire by putting a match to some robes and watching the sleeves burn. She was turned over to juvenile authorities. The career of Charlotte's most daring arsonist, then began—and ended—at age 13.*

So the church arsonist was a child, and one not afraid to admit her deeds.

JIM BAKKER: GREED AND GOD IN A THEME PARK

Jim Bakker is a dynamic, charismatic individual, even after being broken. His ability to raise money and influence people was ten times as strong when he came to Charlotte in the 1980s to set up the PTL (Praise the Lord) Network. With a full head of hair and large framed glasses, he held a microphone easily and commanded a TV screen in increasingly more and more homes in America as his televangelist empire grew and more and more people viewed him as a religious celebrity.

He built a monster church on some farmland in Fort Mill, South Carolina, just over the South Carolina state line from Charlotte, and he looked to Charlotte for much of the funding for his Christian-themed dream. It included housing for the faithful who provided "love offerings" to get into an exclusive club and had a transportation system and various gift shops. In fact, Bakker looked like he was building a Six Flags out there in Fort Mill. And as a matter of fact, building one of the biggest theme parks in the nation is exactly what he was doing. The park, named Heritage USA, was about God, yes, but it was more about entertainment.

Bakker's PTL Network ranked second only to Pat Robertson's CBN (Christian Broadcasting Network), receiving more than $100 million a year, much of which was invested in the 2,300-acre Heritage USA theme park. Heritage USA opened in 1978 and by 1986 was the third largest such enterprise in the country, trailing only Walt Disney World and Disneyland.

There was a roller skating rink (with a patriotic paint scheme inside) where church youth groups from all over the region would come to eat pizza and awkwardly skate in preteen angst. There was a main street of shops patterned after what looked like the Main Street USA in Disney's Magic Kingdom, offering air-conditioned indoor shopping for the Christian consumer. There was a hotel that never was completed that now stands ruined against the Piedmont midsummer sun. And then there were the Christmas lights and the water park.

The Heritage USA Christmas lights were a celebration of the virgin birth in over-the-top twentieth-century American style. The lights were about excess, rows and rows of every kind of Christmas light scene imaginable, from rows of candy canes (although they are not specifically mentioned in the Bible) to images of the manger scene to the wise men crossing the desert in multi-colored twinkly lights. Cars full of people would voluntarily sit in traffic jams for hours to creep through and gawk at the lights, stopping inside the park for some apple cider if they wished.

The Heritage USA lights became a Charlotte tradition to discuss and to see during the holidays, especially for the brand of Christian who subscribed to Bakker's type of charismatic fundamentalist preaching. The Heritage USA phenomenon was evidence of the success of "going with God," how the Savior could sometimes bless those who were doing his work in the here and now with earthly riches. And of course, it was about spreading that message through the magic of Christmas and electricity.

But Bakker and the PTL Club did not just cover this message once a year—no. The Heritage USA family meant to permeate the landscape with its message of Christian entertainment, and although there were rolling rinks and flashing candy canes, summer was lacking the PTL influence. So Bakker and his groupies raised massive amounts of money to build a Heritage USA water park, an arm of the Heritage USA enterprise but one requiring a separate entrance and a separate fee to enter. It was a wonderful theme park and provided threatening competition to Carowinds, a Charlotte institution, just a few miles down Interstate 77.

The waterpark was simply impressive. There was a tidal pool, complete with wave machine, manmade grottoes and lagoons, tube rides, waterslides and a massive flume slide that made national news when Jerry Falwell slid down the vertical drop in a suit a few years later after acquiring the property. The water wonderland was packed during the summer, children and families filling the rides and dropping lots of cash at the snack bar and video arcades. If this was Christian, it sure was fun, and a lot more fun than the confessional box or penances in other Christian denominations. This was being redeemed at its best, and it was full of waves, waterslides and sun.

But Jim Bakker did not build his empire as a lonely man. He had his wife, Tammy Faye, by his side. A heavily made up blonde woman with bright blue eyes and a quavering singing voice, she was right by his side with the musical selection for each broadcast of the PTL Club, microphone and handkerchief in hand. Her mascara-covered eyes would grow dewy at least once a show and her voice would crack as she sang or spoke about God's goodness. And His goodness was evident to all television viewers as she raised her hand in praise, a hand festooned with rings and gold bracelets, nails manicured and painted.

Tammy Faye was fond of many things besides singing, and standing by her man was one of them (at least until he went to jail). The Bakkers were reputed to have an air-conditioned doghouse and gold bathroom fixtures in their lakeside parsonage, but these were rumors and reports after the financial scandal. However, it was known that Tammy Faye liked to visit the Metrolina Flea Market on the northern outskirts of Charlotte, wearing a fur coat in the mild Charlotte winters, shopping with an entourage in the dusty stalls for antiques.

But beneath this slick televangelist exterior, this couple was in marital trouble, with infidelity looming on the horizon, an infidelity that would eventually train investigative eyes on the PTL empire and reveal both sexual and financial scandals, bringing down one of the largest Christian organizations in the South.

JESSICA HAHN

There are conflicting stories about Jessica Hahn, and even though there were formal investigations, the truth about her background is a little fuzzy. What is the truth is that Hahn was working as a church secretary in 1980 and that she idolized Jim Bakker. There was a man in the PTL organization named John Fletcher who knew Hahn, and he arranged for Hahn to travel to Clearwater, Florida, where Jim and Tammy were holding a revival.

The young secretary with the red hair was only twenty-one at the time, and she was well put together by anyone's standards. She had an easy smile and an easy manner, and although she still asserts that all she did was walk her dog and go to church, it was clear that she saw Jim Bakker as a rock star evangelist, complete with fame and a three-piece suit. She also mentioned that she used to watch the show for hours each day, wanting to be a part of the Bakker family. It was obvious that she wanted to be a part of the Bakker's inner circle, but she did not realize how infamous a part she was to become.

Hahn was supposed to baby-sit for the Bakkers, according to her account of the incident on *Larry King Live*, but when she met Jim in her hotel room at the Sheraton Sand Key Resort, it was clear that she was not there to baby-sit.

> *HAHN: But what I'm trying to say is that he—they arranged for me to come to Clearwater, Florida, to watch their children. We waved. We said hello. Jim Bakker walks in with his little itty-bitty shorts. He rips up the bedspread. He takes off my dress. And he lays me down on the bed.*
>
> *I had never had sex until then. And what I'm trying to say is that this guy—you know, it's typical preachers. They get a Bible, and they get a microphone, they got a three-piece suit.*
>
> *KING: Why didn't you hate him and report it? I know you were attached to the church.*

WICKED CHARLOTTE

HAHN: Because you know why? You know why? Because my whole life was the church. And I didn't want people to—you know, you know how many people's lives—he had his own zip code. He had his own post office box. This man had an empire.

Hahn accused Bakker and "the middle man" John Fletcher of drugging her before the incident, and also accused Fletcher of raping her after Bakker had. She said she "had blood coming out of my back. And you know, he [Fletcher] just went nuts on me."

This case did not become public until eight years later when the *Charlotte Observer* got wind of the news through an insider tip that Hahn said was from John Fletcher himself. Although Hahn received hush money for the incident, she said that she did not reveal the incident at the time because she did not want to take down the church. She did not know exactly what to do since she had been a virgin at the time of the incident and was in her words "very green."

Bakker's details provide a very different version of events.

The evangelist said that Hahn was not a virgin and it was not rape. It was consensual sex, and according to Bakker, Hahn "was a professional." But neither party denied a sexual encounter, and later Tammy Faye was accused of infidelity before Bakker's encounter with Hahn. Clearly, this was not a perfect couple living in a perfect world, but two people caught up in a scandal of sex and money, although Tammy Faye was innocent of much of the embezzlement to come.

However, Hahn did not stay in her pseudo-virginal-victim-secretary role long when the spotlight of infamous celebrity took hold of her life. She "escaped" to the lavish mansion of *Playboy* founder Hugh Hefner, who "became her new church." She started a second life as a soft-core porn star and *Playboy* pinup, appearing as a *Playboy* cover in September of 1988. She then had a famous involvement with comedian Sam Kennison and starred in his music video for "Wild Thing."

Wanting to continue her newfound fame, she then decided to launch an acting career, but a church secretary whose only acting credits came from press conferences was not the first name on a callback list for many auditions. However, she eventually landed a role on the television show *Married...With Children*, met the show's creator Ron Leavitt and they are still together, living in Los Angeles, fifteen years later.

SCOUNDRELS, CADS AND MISBEHAVING WOMEN

The Money Scandal

"By the time it all came tumbling down, the PTL Inspirational Network and Heritage Village in nearby Fort Mill, South Carolina, boasted 600,000 regular supporters, an annual income of $129 million, and physical assets approaching $100 million," said Grant Wacker, associate professor of religious studies at the University of North Carolina, who was writing about the scandal in 1989.

See, the sex scandal was only the beginning, and Hahn revealed that she only admitted it after she was sure that it was going to come out in the press. Behind the scenes, investigators had been looking into the PTL Network for years, and there were allegations that rival televangelist Jerry Falwell had hired investigators to discredit PTL in order to gain control of the television empire. Whether or not this was entirely true, the investigators did find wrongdoing and Jerry Falwell eventually took control of PTL. Wacker detailed what the investigators found:

> The one that proved most lucrative and, ultimately, contributed most to Bakker's undoing was the Lifetime Partnership program, launched in 1983. The exact terms varied month to month, but the basic principle remained constant. For a substantial sum — usually $1,000 — contributors were guaranteed several nights' lodging in the posh Heritage Grand Hotel or Heritage Towers (the latter was never built), as well as other perks, each year for the rest of their lives. "New projects pay for old," became the watchword. And it worked. All told, some 114,000 followers paid nearly $170 million for the Lifetime partnerships — a figure several times more than was needed to put up the hotels, and numbers far more than the hotels ever could have accommodated.
>
> Besides the Big Swindle on the Partnerships, there were countless "little" indiscretions that regularly turned up among the PTL top brass. As Jim and Tammy pleaded with the faithful to give their all, Jim and Tammy did their best to spend their all: $25,000 for a face lift for Jim; $8,500 for an anniversary bash at a Charlotte restaurant; $10,000 for a shopping spree in New York; $100,000 for a whim-of-the-moment chartered flight to California; and on and on, all from PTL coffers. When it

was over the IRS would claim that between 1981 and 1989 the Bakkers had received some $9 million in excess compensation from the tax-exempt organization.

Add to that Bakker's repeated sexual indiscretions with men and the sexual scandal with Jessica Hahn, and it seemed that the main villain in all this, although there were definitely some supporting players, was Jim Bakker himself. Known as charismatic and boyish on camera, he was arrogant and distant off-camera. For a man who had grown up in abject poverty in Minnesota, with no inside toilet until he was eight, he was a man who started to equate his longing and declarations with the will of God. He surrounded himself with very smart "lieutenants," men who had been successful in the outside world, but who became strangely loyal to his methods and schemes once inside the PTL confines.

Jim Bakker was tried by Judge Potter in Charlotte and sentenced to a $500,000 fine and forty-five years in prison. Tammy divorced him, and his massive Christian empire bled into the hands of Jerry Falwell and then into the ground of the farmland on which it had been created. It now sits as a wasteland of rotting buildings and cracked concrete as a testament to greed and overindulgence. The place itself is covered with a pariah vibe, and the property, though expansive and possibly lucrative, lies vacant, no one seriously wishing to take on the enormous job of cleaning up both the property itself and its reputation.

Wacker asserts that although Bakker was an embezzler and a liar, he was more significant than that:

How a small-town boy with little more than a high-school education and next to no business skill could persuade hundreds of thousands of believers to fork over more than a half-billion dollars surely places Bakker among the heavyweight hucksters of all time.

And that is the key point. Bakker was a huckster, not a charlatan. The judge and jury said otherwise, I realize. Yet I wonder if they realized to what extent Bakker offered countless small-town Pentecostal and evangelical Christians a taste of glitz, a taste of the good life they themselves were never able to afford, or if they were, never able to enjoy without feeling both out of place and more than a bit guilty. True enough, toward the end things got badly mixed up. But if PTL became more a resort for saints than a hospital for sinners, it would not be the first time — nor the last — that perfectionist Christians found out that the road to perfection is pitted with perils.

JEANETTE LARK: A PUBLIC PROSTITUTE

Prostitution is famously known as "the oldest profession in the world," but it was definitely not something that polite Southern society discussed. In Charlotte, with its numerous hotels and streets stretching out into the county, prostitution had more places to go. And with the money that flowed through Charlotte, prostitution was inevitable.

Still, when the *Charlotte Observer* approached new reporter Charles Kuralt to do a story on prostitution in 1955, this polite Southern gentleman who ultimately would become a household name was not necessarily keen on the idea. He tentatively investigated and then declared that there was no prostitution in Charlotte. How could there be with its well-clad ladies walking briskly down the sidewalks to Belk's or the pharmacy, or the men in fedoras tipping their hats in hello or walking by a ball field where children were running around the bases?

However, when the newspaper did not like Kuralt's initial answer, he came back with a rare gem — instead of a general exposé on prostitution in Charlotte, Kuralt told the story of one prostitute, high-priced Jeanette Lark, who was open about her lifestyle and the money she received from it. In a Southern city like Charlotte, Lark's story is remarkable, not necessarily because of her prostitution, but because she was not famous or notorious, just a minor criminal whose infamous legacy was recorded by Kuralt to stand the test of time. It gives us a glimpse inside the repression of the 1950s, and, frankly, where that repression ran, seemingly right into the arms of Jeanette Lark or someone like her, ready and with money to spend.

"Sometimes I made way over $100 a night," Jeanette Lark testified from the witness chair. One week, she said, she made $1,000.

The pretty, married brunette said she plied her trade for almost a year at two local hotels. She gave 40 percent of her income to two bellboys, James and Will Ely, she testified. They allegedly arranged her "dates" for her.

Jeanette Lark made the headlines.

Service was stellar in Charlotte hotels in the 1950s, especially if she was plying her trade in a downtown establishment. The halls would be cool and the bellhops discreet, especially if they were getting paid under the table.

KU KLUX KLAN: REARING ITS UGLY HEAD EARLY

The Ku Klux Klan was formed after the Civil War as a response to Reconstruction in the South. Although there has been much debate about why it was started, it nevertheless evolved into an honest-to-goodness terrorist organization that secretly met all over the South and systematically terrorized the African American population. Cross burning, whipping and lynchings are all unfortunately part of the American consciousness, and the KKK or some form of it was often responsible for these outbreaks of racial rage within Southern communities.

Although Charlotte has usually been seen as a town without major racial tensions (the city generally accepted segregation because it was good for business and had one of the first school busing programs in the country), that does not mean that Charlotte was free from racially motivated crime. In fact, soon after the War Between the States ended, a man named H.C. Luce settled a few miles outside of Charlotte and decided to set up a business. *Harper's Weekly*, a national magazine with a huge readership, ran an editorial about Luce and the situation that ensued, connecting the words "Charlotte" with "Klansman" for thousands of readers:

Mr. H.C. Luce, in the winter of 1869, went with some friends and settled in Western North Carolina, near Charlotte. They established iron-works, spending, of course, a great deal of money, employed hundreds of poor whites and poorer blacks, opening up markets, and doing precisely what North Carolina needs to have done. They took no part in politics, and asked for no office, but being seven miles from any town or regular church or school, at the request of some of their colored laborers they opened a Sunday-school for both blacks and whites. Admiral Wilkes's rich plantation was near by, and he and his family were also educating the people, and built a little church, to which they invited a clergyman, who had been a rebel soldier.

This community, out in the county west of Charlotte (a part of the county that was later redrawn as Gaston County), was quietly integrating for the good of the ironworks and the people who profited from it. Whether it was the invitation of a clergyman who had fought for the Confederacy, or whether it was some other factor, nevertheless, racist eyes suddenly gazed upon the ironworks and decided that the situation had to be stopped.

The colored workmen of the Admiral were attacked and whipped, their school-books and Bibles were burned, and the clergyman was warned to leave or he would be murdered.

Those who know Admiral Wilkes can judge whether he was likely to permit any thing that could be considered unfairly exciting, and Mr. Luce's veracity is amply attested. The result of the attempt at civilization was the appearance of the Ku-Klux, and the consequent terror, scourgings, and burnings. Mr. Luce himself was menaced with mobbing, as inciting the colored men to retaliation; and most of the Democrats in the neighborhood excused the crimes as only punishing those deserving of punishment. At last, of course, Mr. Luce and his friends were driven away, and one of the most reasonable and promising efforts at settlement and industrial development in one of the late rebel States was violently ended, upon no plea whatever but that the laborers were peacefully instructed in schools where two things were required — that the races should not be taught together, and that politics should be excluded.

This barbarism, which is the work of Southern Democrats, and which indefinitely delays real reconstruction, is sustained by the Northern Democratic press, which sneers at the Ku-Klux as a mere hobgoblin, and denies the truth of such tales as this of Mr. Luce. And whether the Southern Democracy intends to acquiesce in equal rights every body will judge for himself.

In the Charlotte area as elsewhere throughout the South, the official government and even the Northern press refused to acknowledge the presence of the Ku Klux Klan, calling it a figment of imagination or a "hobgoblin." Therefore, unequal treatment continued and even worsened, and then was eventually translated officially through Jim Crow laws, which gripped the South in a stranglehold until the 1960s.

But this was not an isolated incident in a western part of Mecklenburg County. The other figure mentioned in the *Harper's Weekly* editorial had been fighting against slavery for years, and the ironworks was simply an excuse for retaliation against those efforts.

ADMIRAL CHARLES WILKES

Rear Admiral Charles Wilkes is the stuff of high school history books — literally. A resident of Charlotte who joined the Union and became estranged from his son John, Wilkes became famous on November 8, 1861, when he commanded the crew of the USS *Jacinto* to stop the British steamer *Trent* and arrest two Confederate diplomats. The seizure and internment of the two diplomats brought Great Britain to the brink of war with the United States, that is, until Secretary of State William Steward got involved and brought the whole "Trent Affair" to a peaceful close.

In 1964, Wilkes was court-marshaled for insubordination and conduct unbecoming an officer and after serving a sentence, he retired from the U.S. Navy in 1866.

However, from 1838 to 1842, Wilkes commanded the U.S. Surveying and Exploration Expedition, being the first to cite Antarctica as a separate continent. He also toured the South Pacific and the West Coast of the United States.

So how did a larger-than-life man end up in rural Mecklenburg County and later as part of a *Harper's Weekly* editorial on Reconstruction in the South?

After the war, Wilkes decided to move back to North Carolina, specifically to the High Shoals property, in anticipation of a railroad passing through that land. He speculated that an ironworks would

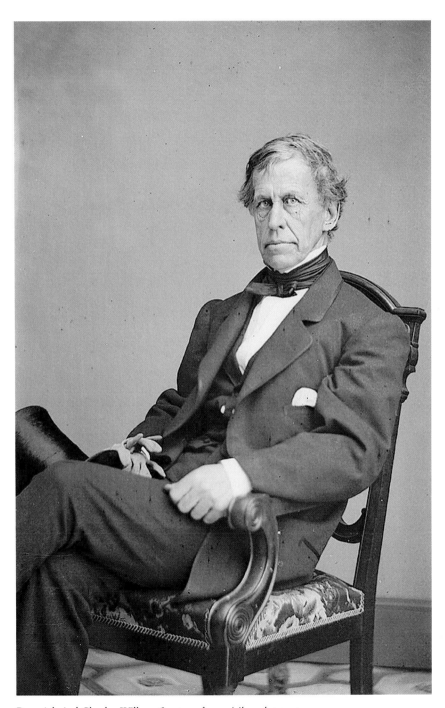

Rear Admiral Charles Wilkes. *Courtesy of www.civilwarphotos.net.*

secure his family's future, and with his wife and daughters, moved to the 14,000-acre property. However, this business venture was a failure, what with scheming business partners and ironworks producing large amounts in the Great Lakes region and Richmond, Virginia. Plus, there was the whole freeman's business, which led to the racist rebuke. Barbara Brose, retired director of the Gaston County Museum of Art and History, has researched Wilkes extensively and noted his employment of freedmen:

> *Wilkes' employment of freedmen and the establishment of a Freedmen's School at High Shoals was entirely consistent with his convictions: and a contrast to his son John's enslavement, purchase and sale of blacks to run the Charlotte operations through the 1860s. Indeed it also appears entirely consistent with efforts of John's wife, Jane Renwick Smedburg Wilkes, who is remembered as the "Godmother of North Carolina Hospitals." She had helped nurse Civil War wounded, and later as an officer of the parish Church Aid Society, raised funds to establish the Charlotte Home and Hospital. It opened in 1876—the first civilian hospital in the state. Later she helped found Good Samaritan Hospital, one of the nation's first hospitals built for blacks. One can only imagine the conversation at the Wilkes family table in High Shoals.*
>
> *From the beginning Charles Wilkes had been unable to repay his High Shoals loans. In the Wilkes family papers, preserved at the Library of Congress, one finds an array of dismaying warrants, deeds, and foreclosure threats. And in Gaston County, Deed Book #5 lists outstanding debts in 1873 in the amounts of $30,000, $4,000, $25,000—all due in sixty days! By the end, Wilkes was able to sign over only the High Shoals house and contents to his wife and adult daughters. After the loss of the High Shoals property in 1874, a discouraged and ailing Wilkes moved back to Washington DC. There he died on February 8, 1877 at the age of 78. A pending Bill of Relief for the payment of his debts was passed by the Senate shortly thereafter.*

KKK'S SEPTEMBER OF 1957

It was 1957. Elvis had already appeared on the Ed Sullivan show. Rosa Parks had already been arrested in Mississippi for not giving up her seat on the bus. And in Charlotte, the Visualite Theatre on Elizabeth Avenue, now a music venue, was still a movie theatre and had a booked screening of *Island in the Sun.*

Island in the Sun was set on a fictitious Caribbean island, and it was the story of a young, handsome black male with political aspirations. Starring Harry Belafonte and Dorothy Dandridge along with Joan Fontaine and Joan Collins, it featured a brief on-screen interracial kiss.

As is the case in so many protests of this type, most of the protestors had simply heard about the content, not actually viewed the material themselves, and rumors ran wild about the movie. Charlotteans were not the only people to experience protests of the movie, but the movie caused something rare to happen in Mecklenburg County: the supposedly non-existent Ku Klux Klan came out in all its hooded glory to protest in front of the Visualite Theatre, right on Elizabeth Avenue, right in the heart of the city.

Although the KKK was not strong in number in front of the theatre, they nevertheless were organized. Their signs were professionally lettered and declared formally that they were protesting the showing of *Island in the Sun.*

That brought Chief of Police Littlejohn down to Elizabeth Avenue, but the Klansmen dispersed without incident when asked to do so. There was another Klan event scheduled that day, not for Elizabeth Avenue but for the steps of the Mecklenburg County Courthouse.

Dr. Dan Morrill noted what also happened on that first day in September 1957:

> *Even more provocative and outlandish were comments made by a racist rabble-rouser named John Kasper. Having already enflamed racial passions among whites in Winston-Salem and Greensboro, Kasper came to Charlotte on September 1st and signed up members for what he called the White Citizens Council. He delivered an inflammatory speech to about 300 white people who had gathered on the steps of the Mecklenburg County*

Courthouse. He called upon the white citizens of Charlotte to rise up against the school board. "We want a heart attack, we want nervous breakdowns, we want suicides, we want flight from persecution," Kasper declared. Aware that native-born evangelist Billy Graham was scheduled to arrive from New York City the next day, Kasper said: "Billy Graham left here a white man but he's coming back a n——— lover." Billy Graham, a man of impeccable character and highest standing in Charlotte and the nation as a whole, declined to respond to such ridiculous dribble when he stepped off the train at the Southern Railroad Station on September 2nd.

All of this was leading up to the big day, September 4, 1957, when Charlotte schools were integrating for the first time. Under pressure of integration, Arkansas Governor Orval Faubas had already surrounded his school with National Guardsmen and declared the school off-limits. On September 5, Dorothy Counts, whose father taught theology at Johnson C. Smith, was dropped off in front of Harding High School and bravely walked the sidewalk past a crowd of white people who spit on her, threw things at her feet and jeered with ugly mouths. The pictures of the poised Counts and jeering whites were splashed all over the country's newspapers and even the *New York Times*. The shame this brought to Charlotte's business leaders was palatable. Charlotte suddenly had an ugly sticker upon its business vest. Morrill wrote, "The greatest legacy of the stirring events that had transpired at Harding High School on September 4, 1957, was the determination of Charlotte's business leaders that such events would never happen again."

Although Charlotte did integrate peacefully for the most part, the city was not without its racial violence, even after its racial tensions had reared their ugly head in the national news.

THE TARGETING OF JULIUS CHAMBERS

Julius Chambers was born in Mount Gilead, North Carolina, in 1936. He learned early about racism when his father did mechanic work for a white man who refused to pay him. From an early age, he decided that he wanted to become a lawyer to fight such injustice. And this was a man that did just what he set out to do, no matter what obstacles lay ahead of him.

He began law school at the University of North Carolina at Chapel Hill in 1959, where he was the first African American editor in chief of the school's law review. Upon graduating in 1962, Chambers ranked first in his class of one hundred students and went on to earn his LL.M. from Columbia University Law School in 1964.

Soon after he started his own law firm in Charlotte, which later became the first integrated law firm in North Carolina. He fought for civil rights all along the way, eventually winning the landmark case *Swann v. Charlotte-Mecklenburg Schools* in 1971. This case led to federally mandated busing and fueled integration all throughout the country.

That case alone, not to mention the history of cases leading to that one, ignited a lot of racial backlash in Charlotte. Some of that backlash led to citizens pulling their children out of the public school system, then creating private schools that were exempt from the new laws. But retaliation took a deadlier form when it turned personal against Chambers.

Despite his North Carolina schooling and involvement in the local community, Chambers nevertheless became a target for a series of planned attacks against him. At least three direct acts were committed against Chambers or his family, and yet no one was injured:

On November 22, 1965, the homes of four civil rights leaders— Julius Chambers, Fred Alexander, Kelly Alexander and Reginald Hawkins—were bombed in Charlotte. Chambers's car had already been exploded with dynamite in New Bern, North Carolina, and this was just some of the violence his family endured. One bomb went off in the bedroom of an eight-year-old, but unbelievably, no one was injured in the blast. No one was ever charged with the crimes.

Prior to January 1971, the father of Julius Chambers owned an auto repair shop. In 1971, it was burned down. Chambers once again was a target for violence, since he was the lawyer on a landmark Charlotte desegregation case.

On February 4, 1971, the law office of Julius Chambers was burned down. Chambers and others asserted that the assault was in direct correlation to Chambers arguing *Griggs v. Duke Power*, a discrimination case in which Duke Power was accused of using a test to prevent black employees from being promoted. The case sparked new laws concerning employee rights.

Chambers was unharmed from these incidents. In fact if anything, they seemed to strengthen his resolve that he was on the right path. He went on to serve as part of the North Carolina Board of Governors, then served as the chancellor of North Carolina Central University for eight years.

NOTORIOUS MURDERERS AND THEIR EVIL DEEDS

THE MURDER OF FRANCIS BRADLEY: THE STRONGEST PATRIOT

Mecklenburg County (and the battles that surrounded it, including King's Mountain) was a decisive piece of geography for the cause of American Patriotism during the Revolutionary War. When the British came into the county, they declared it was a "hornet's nest" and thus, the hornet's nest became a symbol for Charlotte and its surrounding county.

One of the brightest "hornets" in the nest was Francis Bradley. The sheriff of Mecklenburg County, he was a staunch Patriot who was said to be the strongest man in the county. Physically imposing in nature, he was even more impressive on his horse. He was known as someone with a cool head and confident courage. He was the son-in-law of James Alexander, one of the signers of the Mecklenburg County Declaration of Independence, thus putting him in the middle of one of the most prominent families in the Charlotte area.

Just as the Civil War would divide the land not a century later, the War for American Independence divided communities into Whigs (Patriots) and Tories (those remaining loyal to the British crown). Since Charlotte was a hotbed for the Whigs, it was only natural it became a target for the Tories. However, four Tories were not interested in remaining loyal to the British crown. They wanted to go home and were not loyal enough to any cause to prevent them from waiting another day.

Colonel Samuel Bryan, a prominent Tory leader, was on his retreat from Charlotte near Old Nations Ford in November of 1780. Four of his men, John and Richard McCombs and a Mr. Ridge and Mr. Griffin, decided to desert. They had had enough of retreating, and they were looking possibly to return to their homes in Surry County, North Carolina. The tide of the Revolution had turned in Mecklenburg County, and although these men did not know it at the time, they did know that their retreat was an embarrassing defeat that was still smarting in their brains long after the battles.

Nevertheless, the men knew that desertion would not be looked upon favorably. They also would have to travel through Whig country to get there. So the men devised a plan to travel the roads during the night and hide in the thickets beside the roads during the day.

On November 14, 1780, the men were hiding in a thicket a mile from Colonel Francis Bradley's home, the strongest man in the county.

About midday, the imposing man got his gun and set out to look for some missing cattle. In his search, he found much more than the cattle. He came upon two men who looked to be up to no good, and in that time of war, he was inclined to believe that that is what they were up to. So he began questioning them, and after a few minutes, took them prisoner. He was, after all, the sheriff. W.A. Graham recounted in his book, *General Joseph Graham and His Papers on North Carolina Revolutionary History*, what happened next:

> *The other two, who had been lying about twenty steps off, and whom he had not seen, came behind him and seized him; a violent scuffle ensued, until one of them got his own gun and shot him dead. Bradley was a very stout man, and with out weapons would have been a match for all four of them; a man of cool and deliberate courage, much respected by all who knew him, and his death much regretted.*

But the story was not over. A few weeks later, Richard McCombs and Griffin were killed, and the other two men taken to the Salisbury jail in Rowan County. The men were questioned about the alleged murder of

Francis Bradley, and it was then that the desertion plot unraveled even further. John McCombs, brother of the slain Richard, turned state's evidence and implicated his accomplice Mr. Ridge. Although Ridge's first name has been lost from Graham's account, the account of his death was not. Ridge was hanged for the murder of Francis Bradley, the only one to be punished by the emerging state for his involvement in the murder of the strongest Whig in Mecklenburg County.

Hanging was the preferred method of execution in North Carolina until 1910, and the hanging in Salisbury probably followed a prescribed pre-execution ritual. The rope would be oiled to make sure that the knot slid easily and then the pull weight and trap door would be tested. When the rope was placed around the prisoner's neck, it would be slipped behind the left ear, hopefully providing an instantaneous death. If any of these rituals were missed, the results would even be more gruesome than a "smooth" hanging. The damned would swing and suffocate for minutes or hours, and if the weight was too heavy, it could result in decapitation. On that day in Salisbury, no doubt that Ridge was recalling the thicket in which he hid along a dirt road in Mecklenburg County, and the murder that had occurred in broad daylight. We can only hope his was a quick death, for we have no account to the contrary.

W.J. CASH: SUICIDE OR MURDER?

This is not a straight story of murder. The death of W.J. Cash is shrouded in mystery, even sixty-five years after his death. Although his death has been and still is officially ruled suicide, the events surrounding that death are strange and unusual at the least. If W.J. Cash took his own life, then he did so at a most crucial time in his literary career for which he had strived so adamantly. If his life was taken, we will never know, for there was no official autopsy of his remains and only a hasty investigation by the Mexican police. But he was an important figure in Charlotte at the time of his death and a rising star on the national literary scene.

Even today, W.J. Cash is a pioneer in the literary world. His groundbreaking book, *The Mind of the South*, was very important in the study of Southern literature and the idea of "the South" in general. To top this, he was a regular columnist for the *Charlotte News* as its assistant editor. He was a local celebrity, a noted literary figure and a cultural theorist.

Cash and his wife moved in somewhat glamorous circles, especially literary ones. It was 1941, *Gone With the Wind* was still reverberating in the American consciousness and W.J. and his wife, Mary Cash Maury, shared a friendship with the Atlantan author, Margaret Mitchell. Cash and his wife had recently visited Mitchell and her husband in Atlanta in March of 1941 and enjoyed drinks with them at the old Piedmont Driving Club. There, Mitchell and Cash discussed "Tara," what it was really like in the Old South and enjoyed some good Scotch. Mary recalled that "it was delightful."

Upon returning to Charlotte, the couple found out that Cash had received a Guggenheim Fellowship with a year's allowance of $2,000, enough for him to go away to write a novel. Since Europe was at war with the Nazis, the couple decided on Mexico where their money could go further and they could mix business with a long-delayed honeymoon.

Although they had not announced their plans yet to anyone, the couple then received a brochure for an inn in Guadalajara, and joked at the time about the Nazis having a plot against Cash. He had written many anti-Nazi editorials over the years, and although he was a writer in Charlotte, Charlotte was still for the most part a sleepy town and really not feasible as a blip on the Nazis' map. Nevertheless, Mary said that it was certainly a joke, but later, she wondered if he had taken that joke and filed it away in his mind, only to bring it up in a twisted way at a later time.

The couple did not decide to stay at the inn in Guadalajara, but instead in Mexico City. Cash had received an invitation to speak at the University of Texas's commencement address, and all seemed to be working out fine—the honorarium would make their trip worthwhile.

So they set out for Mexico, and on the train, Mary recalled later in *The Red Clay Reader*, the author began to exhibit erratic behavior:

> *On the train to Texas he had a curious and violent fit of anger, stamping a newspaper on the floor and biting his hands. It was quickly over, but he could not remember what caused it and I was puzzled and alarmed.*

Although the speech was considered well spoken by many, Cash did not seem to think so, and this added to the ill feelings he was already having as the couple traveled south of the border. Both members of the party were having some stomach ailments, and Cash especially was experiencing some culture shock once they settled into their apartment in Mexico City. Then came the night of June 30, a night that, even as Mary recalled it in 1967, seemed to chill her in recollection:

> *Cash asked me if I could hear those people talking outside. We were sitting in our small foyer dining room which gave onto the street entrance of the apartment house. We had often heard people talking in the hallway outside, and I assumed he was hearing them now. He did not then show any fear, only seemed to be deliberately and intently eavesdropping. Then he started whispering the substance of their talk: they were Nazis planning to kill one or both of us. I stood as still as I have ever stood...I tried to reason with him. I didn't hear any voices, and, if he would think for a moment, he would realize that he didn't either.*

Cash later picked up a butcher knife to defend himself against whoever might walk through that door. It was only after much persuasion that Mary convinced him to put the knife down. Then the couple got ready for bed and Cash requested that she read from the book of Ecclesiastes.

Now, these are the classic symptoms of schizophrenia: paranoia and the hearing of voices. But before history rules out Cash's ranting as that of a crazy individual, history must also confess that 1941 Mexico City was a hotbed for Nazis. In fact, there was a pipeline of black-market Texas oil traveling through Mexico to the Nazi army. Now, did the Nazis read the *Charlotte News* or any of Cash's other publications? Who knows. But were they extremely thorough and organized enough to read all American anti-Nazi sentiment? Yes. And would Nazis residing in Mexico City have known about Cash's close proximity? Sounds likely.

Mary was only going to have one more day with her husband. On July 1, 1941, she reported that he was himself again and that he apologized for his behavior the night before and readily agreed to see a doctor later that day at 2:00 p.m. When Mary returned from a neighbor's house where she had made the appointment, Cash was nowhere to be seen, but when he returned, he started his ranting about the Nazis again, and only after much persuasion was Mary able to get the pale and shaking Cash to the doctor.

At the doctor's, he refused help, very much "in a state," and when Mary wanted to look elsewhere for help, Cash insisted that she not use the telephone, as the Nazis would intercept the call. So Cash insisted that Mary go out for help while Cash locked himself in their room. When Mary returned with a man from the Associated Press, Ben Meyer, Cash was gone. They started searching for him in different hotels, but it was not until nearly 10:00 p.m. that they called a hotel that said he was registered. Both Meyer and Mary set out for the hotel.

What Mary saw next she saw for only a moment, but it was ingrained in her brain forever:

> *My knock on Cash's door got no answer. The hotel manager, standing in the van of what I recall as a horde of silent people, refused to open the door but handed me the key. I entered the room and saw Cash hanging from the open bathroom door. He had been dead for several hours, it was later found. My scream brought the crowd inside.*

Within days, Mary had his body cremated in Mexico, for she could not bear "being aware of the baggage car" carrying Cash's body on the long train trip back to North Carolina. Therefore, a proper autopsy could not be performed on the dead author, and the Mexican police seemed satisfied with the suicide ruling. But Mary, in her own words, did not have so simple of an answer.

> *From the time the Nazi story first began to unfold, Cash, a historian, had been able to see the whole picture while only bits of its detail were coming to light. Where the usual early reactions had been uneasiness at the situation in Europe, Cash's emotions had been bloodily torn in rage and horror, in fear from the trend of history, and in frustration at his own helplessness in the face of catastrophe no one seemed to be doing anything forceful to prevent. He had been writing savagely anti-Nazi editorials for years, he had been all but affixed to the radio for the news reports that were always bad, always left him biting his hands. It was not until the war actually began that he gained a balance, calmly finished his long-neglected book, took a wife, relaxed, looked about him*

and found that much of living was really a very fine thing after all. Remembering these things, it seemed to me (in my layman's terms) that all the seemingly forgotten but apparently only submerged pressures had been released by his general malaise during that unsettled month in Mexico, and the result had been an explosion of the mind. Professional analyses have since been made of possible physiological causes of his eventual breakdown and I freely concede that they may be completely accurate, but to me they have no meaning. Until that final month, in the years I had known him he did not seem to be a sick man either to me or to himself.

So Mary conceded that he in fact did commit suicide, but that it was really a result of the Nazi march against Europe. Other experts have loosely suggested that this might have been a framed suicide when it was in reality a Nazi plot, as Cash so vehemently proclaimed. Either way, the world was devoid of a bright Southern literary star not yet cresting his orbit.

HENRY LOUIS WALLACE: THE CHARLOTTE STRANGLER

Henry Louis Wallace was much more than just a criminal. He was a devil in the midst, striking out against familiar faces and those who trusted him. A serial killer who confessed of his crimes in 1994 and now sits on death row, his is a story of an atypical pattern that stumped Charlotte police for almost two years.

Wallace grew up in Barnwell, South Carolina, and it seems that his "problems" with women stemmed from the horrible treatment from his mother. Living in a house that boasted no plumbing or electricity, he had a mother who routinely beat them and generally terrorized Wallace and his sister Yvonne. If she was too tired when she came home from work, she ordered the children to beat one another while she watched. Wallace reported in his social profile before the trial that this type of punishment was worse than receiving a beating himself.

Despite his horrible home situation, Wallace nevertheless graduated from Barnwell High in 1983, and he was respected around the school.

After his mom forbade him to try out for the football team, he joined the cheerleading squad, and the girls on the squad liked him for his polite manner and good attitude. Wallace had school spirit.

However, although his future looked bright after high school, promise soon turned to disappointment. He got a job as a disc jockey at WBAW, a local radio station, and developed a character called "The Night Rider." Women liked his voice; the radio liked his personality. However, WBAW and Wallace soon parted ways when he was caught trying to steal CDs. With nowhere else to go, he joined the navy, and was an exemplary sailor for eight years.

He married his high school sweetheart and adopted her daughter. He was getting perfect achievement points in the navy (whose records indicate was smarter than many who held his rank), he had a family and he wanted to add to it. When his wife refused to have another baby, the marriage began to fall apart. Then he was caught near the naval base on a breaking-and-entering charge. He was asked to leave the navy, and as soon as he was out of the service, his wife left him.

Then in 1992, he moved to Charlotte to be with his sister and mother. In Charlotte, he dated women and even had a child out of wedlock, but he turned more to drugs than anything else for escape. He didn't care about anything, really—not his job, his family, his future, and the drugs were cracking open doors deep inside his psyche, doors that needed to stay shut.

From 1992 to 1994, nine African American women were raped and killed, and the police treated each murder separately, the cases remaining unlinked for a long time. The rapidity and ferocity of the killings led to an angry panic among the minority community where the murders were occurring, but the police force, though working with a steady purpose, was not prepared to deal with a serial killer whose mode did not fit that of a "typical" serial murderer.

Twenty-nine-year-old Wallace was a man who was able to hide his churning rage from his close friends and relatives, and unlike many serial killers, he killed those who knew him, not strangers who fit a particular profile for which he was searching. Charisse Cotton, professor of criminal justice at the University of North Carolina, stated that many people trusted him. Most of his victims did not know that he was about to kill them even seconds before he committed the act.

This man with the sweet smile and pleasant looks terrorized east Charlotte from 1992 to 1994, raping and killing nine African

American women. He killed his victims usually by strangling them and more often than not raped them. More than a couple of his victims had children and one victim, Michelle Stinson, was found by her two sons, aged one and three. They said that "mommy was sleeping on the floor." She was found in a pool of blood on her kitchen floor, Wallace's only stabbing victim.

Joseph Geringer, who compiled his report from the transcript of Wallace's confession and a copy of the authorized profile of Wallace just before his trial, explained what happened next:

> *During the second week of March, 1994, things began to break open. There would be three more murders in three days, between March 9 and 11, culminating in the identification and arrest of the Charlotte Strangler. As a glut had overtaken Henry Louis Wallace, he went berserk and grew careless. The precautions he had previously taken to hide himself—spacing out the murders, wiping off fingerprints, even bathing some of his victims—were abandoned as he went on a joyride of killing.*

First, Betty Baucom did not report to work at Bojangles restaurant on Central Avenue. This was strange to the manager for two reasons: first, Baucom was dependable and trustworthy, and it wasn't like her to "no call, no show," and second, this was the same restaurant where the very first victim, Catherine Love, had worked before her disappearance. So the manager alerted police, and when the officers got to her apartment, they found her lying facedown on her bed, fully clothed and a towel wrapped like a noose about her neck, She'd been dead for more than twenty-four hours.

The next victim to fall prey to Wallace was Brandi Henderson. Her boyfriend found her dead in her apartment. When police arrived at the scene, they realized that Henderson's apartment was in the same complex as Baucom's. In addition to the woman being strangled and dead, a baby had been assaulted as well. Court records indicate that the baby was still alive and Henderson's boyfriend, Verness Lamar Woods, rescued the baby and called for an ambulance. But Wallace's trail had come to an end—with the police responding to the same apartment complex twice in two days for two strangulations of two African American women, they suspected that the Charlotte

Strangler, perhaps, knew his victims. And, of course, he did. Geringer pieced together the thread of suspicion:

The next day after finding Henderson, Commander Gary McFadden drew his squad together for a meeting early the next morning to compare the notes they had made during their interviews with the deceased women's acquaintances. The results of the reports were enlightening. They indicated that the girls did not seem to know each other—although some had crossed paths—or had never worked or schooled together. The clubs where they socialized were different. But…when asked to list names of people with whom each victim associated, all of the interviewees mentioned in their list the same name: Henry Louis Wallace.

Of the slain women, both Shawna Hawk and Audrey Spain had at one time worked at Taco Bell for the same manager, Henry Wallace.

Valencia Jumper was a good friend of Wallace's sister, Yvonne.

Michelle Stinson would often eat at Taco Bell and chat with Wallace.

Vanessa Mack was the sister of one of Wallace's ex-girlfriends.

Betty Baucom was a friend of Wallace's current girlfriend, Sadie McKnight.

Brandi Henderson was the girlfriend of one of Wallace's pals, Verness Lamar Woods, who found Brandi. In fact, Woods had told the police that Wallace was prone to visit with Brandi while he was at work.

Reaching back into the open case of "missing person" Caroline Love, detectives now realized that Love had also known Wallace well; she had been the roommate of Sadie McKnight, his girlfriend, whom Wallace visited regularly.

The puzzle pieces slid into place perfectly now. When pulling a rap sheet on the sudden suspect, Sergeant McFadden was surprised to find that, as he recalls, "An outstanding warrant was already out for Henry Louis Wallace for having failed to come to court on a recent larceny charge."

"When the police approached Sadie McKnight, she was very taken aback, very surprised that her boyfriend Henry was suspected of being the Charlotte Strangler," adds Charisse Coston. "But, the more she thought about it, the more sense it made. All along, Henry had been giving her presents—bracelets, rings and necklaces—

that sometimes seemed to be very familiar. In retrospect, she now realized that she had been wearing dead girlfriends' jewelry!"

But, still Gary McFadden wondered: Is it all just coincidence? So he knew the women...would he have an alibi? Could it be proven he had been with the victims on the nights they were killed?

And then it came, the evidence McFadden dreamed about. Betty Baucom's car was located, abandoned across town. Swipes of fingerprints found on the trunk lid matched Henry Wallace's file prints.

Police staked out Wallace's residence at the Glen Hollow Apartments on North Sharon Amity Road throughout the evening of March 11, 1994, and Officers Gil Allred and Sid Wright found him at a friend's house, where he was cuffed at approximately 5:00 p.m. on March 12. He was calm, did not put up a fight, but it was the confession later at the Law Enforcement Center in Charlotte that really chilled the city by the calmness with which Wallace relayed his heinous crimes.

Wallace seemingly agreed to a taped confession with no coercion, and according to Geringer, said, "I feel like a big burden has been lifted." He then proceeded to take them murder by murder, through each scene, what he was thinking at the time of murder and what the last words of his victims were. His motive was sex, the control and power over women, and, after that, the money from their apartments, which he used to support his spiraling drug addiction.

"At one point, an investigator told Wallace that he did not seem to be a bad man by nature, and asked him if he thought he might be schizophrenic. 'No,' Wallace answered, 'there's only one Henry—a [bad] Henry,'" reported Geringer.

Wallace was convicted of nine counts of murder and other assorted sexual charges and sentenced to death row, transferred to Central Prison in Raleigh. Of course, an automatic appeal followed, which included a tactic to say that his confession had been coerced. To law enforcement, this was unfathomable, because even during the appeal process, Wallace kept unburdening himself with confession. Geiger explained that

even before his trial, Wallace had confessed to other murders for which he was not charged. Besides the prostitute he had admitted killing in Charlotte, he also claimed to have killed, while in the Navy, a woman named Tashanda Bethea in South Carolina in 1990.

"And there were more," Criminal Justice Professor Charisse Coston informs us. "After his incarceration, he told authorities of others. If all true, the estimated number nears twenty, all murdered across the world while he was on naval duty in various ports of call."

RAE CARRUTH: PRO ATHLETE AND MURDERER FOR HIRE

Rae Carruth was born January 20, 1974, in Sacramento, California, as Raelamar Theotis Wiggins. Many people hope he dies in jail.

Rae Carruth was a professional football player, and not just one of the hardworking guys on the defensive line. No, he played wide receiver, one of the highest profile positions on a football team, the person that might make the big catch or might get the extra yards. Because of this, the name Rae Carruth came up in the media more often than the names of those hardworking defensive linemen. And Rae Carruth loved what the limelight could give him: money, fame and women.

He enjoyed his rookie year in the NFL in 1997. He had made it to the big leagues and joined the Carolina Panthers as a wide receiver. But by 1999, the stress of the good life was getting to him. Carruth was facing money problems, just like many rookie players often do who like to party and play the star. In addition, he was in the final year of his contract with the Carolina Panthers, and his play was often less than stellar; he was attempting a comeback. And finally, one of his girlfriends, Cherica Adams, (and by no means was there only one) had told him that she was pregnant with his baby. He was not thrilled. This was simply one more thing he just did not need.

Donna St. George, a writer for the *Washington Post*, detailed the relationship of Adams and Carruth:

> *The couple met at a summer pool party. Cherica Adams had socialized with other athletes, but when she met Carruth, she called her mother, Saundra Adams, and said, "Mom, I've just met my soul mate." That night, she brought him home to meet her father.*
>
> *Their relationship was off and on, however. Cherica Adams went to Atlanta for a time. Carruth had many other girlfriends. In spring 1999, Adams found out she was pregnant — and both of*

them were surprised. Adams took eight home-pregnancy tests before she was convinced, her mother said.

Carruth seemed happy at first, Adams told her mother, but then he asked her to get an abortion. Adams said no.

Once pregnant, she grew to like the idea—playing tapes of Mozart for her fetus, drinking high-protein smoothies and shopping until she acquired a full baby wardrobe from birth to toddler sizes. "She wanted this to be the perfect baby," recalled her mother. "She was forever rubbing her belly and showing us."

The couple's relationship was rocky through much of her pregnancy. Adams "didn't want to just be Number 1 but the only one," her mother said. For a time, they barely talked. Carruth changed his phone number, then took Adams to task for not calling, her mother said. "He kept making and breaking dates," she said. "He was Dr. Jekyll and Mr. Hyde."

At some point, Cherica Adams made it clear she would be seeking child support from Carruth. The prosecutor argued that Carruth was deeply opposed to supporting the child of a woman he was no longer with.

Then in November of 1999, he called to ask her on a "real date." On November 15, 1999, they went to a movie, *The Bone Collector*, full of murder and violent images. Little did Adams know that the movie was only the beginning of her horror for the evening.

During his FBI interview, Carruth stated that while on the date, he told Adams that he considered her a friend, not his girlfriend, although he pointed out that he had been attending some doctor's appointments with her and occasionally giving her money. He said that he told her that it was possible that the baby was his, but that regardless of his doubt, he was going to treat it as one of his own.

After the movie, they were in separate cars on the way to Adams's house. According to prosecutors, Carruth then led Adams down a dark road where he slowed or stopped his SUV, while a car pulled up beside hers and fired into her BMW 325. The 911 tapes that were released after she died tell the next part of the story:

"I've been shot," she said.
"You've been shot?" a 911 operator asked.
"...I'm eight months pregnant," she said.

"…How'd this happen?" a 911 medic inquired.
"I was following my baby's daddy, Rae Carruth, the football player."
"So you think he did it?" the medic asked.
"He slowed down and a car pulled up beside me."
"And then shot at you?" the medic asked.
"Yes."

Police rushed to the scene just minutes after the call, and Adams was alone and bleeding, though still conscious. She told the police the same story that she had relayed to the 911 operator, and then she slipped into a coma. She was rushed to the hospital where her baby, ten weeks premature, was delivered by emergency C-section. A bullet had missed the baby by only one inch.

Adams, twenty-four, died after twenty-eight days in the hospital.

However, the story was not over. Carruth was under suspicion when she died, and suddenly he was missing. The glittering NFL player who at one time so desperately wanted the limelight now was hiding from it. But where?

Carruth, as was mentioned before, was no beggar when it came to girlfriends. Although one had just died from gunshot wounds, there were apparently plenty of other women willing to step in line. Or at least one. Shortly after Carruth learned of Adams's death, he called Wendy Cole, another of his "friends," and begged her to take him to California. He just couldn't face jail again, he said.

He did not make it to California—just as far as the trunk of Cole's car outside a Wildersville, Tennessee, motel. He was arrested, shackled and returned to Charlotte for trial.

With the testimony of the actual shooters implicating Carruth, he was convicted of the murder of Cherica Adams. He had not wanted a "real date" with Adams. He had not wanted a baby. And he definitely had not wanted to pay child support for eighteen years. What he did want was for the situation to go away, and he knew some guys who could do it. Carruth had to play a part too—to ask her out, to keep her calm, to keep them driving separate cars on that fateful night. He played his part wonderfully, but he did not expect his bright football career to end in the darkness of a cramped car trunk in Tennessee. He believed that someone who did not actually shoot the gun could not be convicted of murder. He thought wrong.

APPENDIX

"SIN WITH A SOUTHERN ACCENT"
BY STEPHEN HULL

AUTHOR'S NOTE

I found an original copy of this article in a file of the Robinson-Spangler Carolina Room of the Public Library of Charlotte and Mecklenburg County. The file was "Crime and Criminals," and there was no note about the source from which it was torn. The librarian suggested that the article had probably been mailed to the library as is. Although we were not able to positively identify the magazine, Stephen Hull did write similarly themed articles, one entitled "Baltimore's Bawdy Block," for Stag *magazine in the 1950s. Its views are outdated and its writing very stylized, but it was simply too specific and too wonderfully seedy to omit.*

I got off the train at the old Southern Railway Station in Charlotte on a spring afternoon, and the sweat began rolling down my face. It was hotter than blue blazes, and after the air-conditioned train the heat hit me like a blast from an oven. I'd heard there was a pretty good hotel called the Mecklenburg right across the street from the station, so I staggered out into the sun and sure enough, there it was, looking as cool and inviting as an oasis in the middle of the Sahara. I had no reservation, but fortunately they had a sing with bath available, so I checked in, peeled off my sweaty clothes and dropped gratefully into a cold tub. After that and a cigarette, I was ready for business.

I put in a call to a friend who's a newspaperman in Charlotte. He was a reporter from way back, so I knew he knew where all the bodies were buried.

"Charlie," I said, "I'm in town for a story on Charlotte. Let's have something to eat while you lay it out for me."

"Swell," he said. "But let's get one thing straight. I like it down here. I'd never go back to that rat race in New York. This is my town now, and I like it. But I'll spell it out for you." He mentioned the name of a restaurant. "Grab a cab and meet me there at six."

"How about a drink?" he asked as we sat down at a table for two in the beautifully appointed air-conditioned dining room.

"You mean a real drink? Thought that was taboo down here."

He laughed and turned to the waiter. "Two of the usual."

The waiter brought in two bourbon-on-the-rocks and set them down without saying a word. Charlie lifted his glass: "Success."

We drank and then Charlie began to lay it out. "These Southern towns fool you," he said. "On the surface, everything is clean and quiet except in the colored section, and that isn't supposed to count. This town is 30 percent colored. When you get under the surface a little way, though, you get a different picture. The wool-hat boys from the tobacco plantations and corn field out in the Piedmont don't come into Charlotte on Saturday nights to study their Sunday School lessons. They come in to raise hell, and that means what it does everywhere—liquor, women, and maybe a little gambling, with a fist fight or two on the side."

Charlie went on. "This is only Friday, but I don't have to work tomorrow and I think we can see enough tonight to give you the correct pitch on Charlotte. Things start popping Friday night, anyway—a few of the boys drift in by then. I don't think you'll be disappointed."

It was the understatement of the year. I wasn't disappointed.

Charlie has a new Olds convertible, so we tooled around in style. The first spot was a scabby hotel not far from the Mecklenburg and Southern Station. It was a short cut above a flea-bag, but that was about all. The little lobby was full of men. Most of them wore open-necked suntan shirts and Army-surplus khaki pants. They were lean, tanned.

Many were drinking beer out of the bottle. "Textile workers, most of 'em," said Charlie. "Few peanut-pickers." There were no women in sight.

We walked up to the desk. The clerk was an old man in his shirt sleeves, smoking a cigarette through a long holder.

Charlie said: "Hi George, how's business?"

The old man looked over the top of his glasses at Charlie. "Hello, Chahley. Bizness poh, mighty poh."

"Too bad," said Charlie. "Say George, my friend here would like to see the book."

George looked me over. "We cain't show the registah to strangeahs, Chahley. You know that."

"He's O.K."

George looked at me some more, seemed satisfied that I was all right, and pulled a well-worn photograph album out from beneath the desk. "Suppose you all jes want to look?" he said.

"Just look, not buy," said Charlie.

The book contained a dozen photographs of completely nude girls, each with a name and price—"Jean $10, Emma $15, Helen $5," etc.

I looked at Charlie and he nodded. "You pick a baby, pay your dough, get a key from George here, and go up. She'll be there. She's all yours for half an hour."

We sat around the lobby for about 15 minutes and watched. During that time half a dozen men signed the hotel register, paid for their "room," got a key from George, and walked up the stairs. There was no sign of a woman anywhere.

"It's quiet now," said Charlie. "Along one, two in the morning, when the boys are liquored up, it gets kind of rough. This isn't the only brothel in town, but it's supposed to be the best."

We got back in the Olds and headed down Trade Street tow Tryon. The streets were wide and clean. The town looked good. As we passed a big, block-long Presbyterian church, Charlie said:

"Yep, these Southern cities sure fool you. They say Charlotte is the second greatest church-going city in the world. Edinburgh, Scotland, is the only town that beats it. These Southern towns will out-drink, out-brawl, and out-sex any places their size in the country."

We passed a big department store. Charlie went on: "See that store? It's so strait-laced it won't sell cocktail shakers, whiskey glasses, dice or cards. We've got another big department store down the street. The original owner died a couple of years ago—but when he first started in business he advertised a show sale by driving a cow up the middle of Trade Street with a big sign on it reading 'This is No Bull.' Well, he was a pious Presbyterian layman and he made a standing offer of two dollars to any kid in town who could come into the store and recite the Presbyterian short catechism. His sons—fine boys—are carrying on the business and they've continued the offer. But what the old man didn't know and what the boys don't know is that some of these 'kids' 17, 18 years old, learn the catechism, collect the two bucks, and either use the money for a beer bust or for a woman."

We drove past a garish little theatre. It was advertising a sex movie called "violated!" which, the posters screamed, was "Shocking! Documentary about female and male behavior!" Charlie nodded toward it. "These little scratch houses are introducing a lot of filth into the South that you don't get up North. There isn't any state film censorship down here, which means that local operator can get away with murder. They play these new burlesque movies, and they're bringing the pornography of skid row to Main Street."

Charlie pulled the Olds up in front of a swanky downtown club. "Just want to show you something," he said. We went in. It was a luxuriously furnished businessmen's club with a library, restaurant and other facilities. "Best people in town belong to this club," said Charlie. We went into the club lounge. Banked along the wall were a half dozen slot machines, the same quarter-eating bandits you find in Reno or Las Vegas. They were doing business, too. There was also a roulette wheel, but nobody was playing it at the moment. "Those machines pay the expenses of this club," said Charlie. "But they'll swear there's no gambling in Charlotte."

APPENDIX

Back in the car again, we headed out of the downtown section toward the suburbs. Soon we came to a dusty village made up of long rows of identical four-room houses.

In the warm spring night, shirt-sleeved textile workers were sitting on the tiny porches, smoking and reading their newspapers. It was dreary and depressing. Charlie said: "Places like this — Chadwick-Hoskins, North Charlotte and the rest — are where a lot of the hell in this town is raised. There's nothing much else to do, so the guys drink, fight, gamble, swap wives and girl friends."

This was another Charlotte, strikingly different from the broad, well-kept downtown streets with the impressive new buildings and the lovely old churches. These were the brawling, drinking, gambling company towns, full of girly-girly and cheap bootleg hooch, wide-open and kept that way by shortsighted industrialists.

"Some of these white mill towns are rough," Charlie said. "But they're nothing compared to the colored neighborhoods of Charlotte. Biddleville, Cherrytown, Blue Heaven — they're really rough." He whipped the Olds down a street, and after a while we came to a halt in a rundown, shack-filled, chicken-yard neighborhood called Brooklyn. The place smelled, and the smell wasn't magnolia blossoms.

Charlie had pulled up in front of a big, crude "tabernacle," filled with singing, shouting, sweating people. There was a sign over the door, and I remembered having seen it often in New York's Harlem: WE LOVE YOU, DADDY GRACE. Charlie said; "This is Bishop Grace's church. The fellow does a lot of good. These people are really behind the eight ball down here, but things are getting better. My paper used to have an editor who kept hammering away at the idea that colored people were just as good as anybody and entitled to decent places to live. Few years ago we put on a hell of an exposé of unsanitary housing conditions and the connection between bad housing and immorality. Lot of people uptown didn't like it. Yet, the South is getting educated.

"But," he added, "it's still got a'ways to go."

We spent the rest of the night in Blue Heaven and Cherrytown. Charlie knew a lot of people and they were friendly to him and his paper, because W.J. Cash had gotten the idea across that his paper was in their corner. But even this casehardened reporter, who knows New York's Harlem and Chicago's South Side coming and going, was startled by what he saw in Charlotte's Black Belt. Among the sights turned up in our tour of the district were the following:

A cabaret operating in a lodge hall in Cherrytown, with shake dancers, a real jivey band and whiskey in tea cups. Marijuana ciggies from the old coot who had the men's room concession. Joint ran all night. Patronage half white, half colored.

A cockfight in a pit set up in a backyard in Blue Heaven. In the little lantern-lit arena, about 70 men watched the spurred, blooded cocks tear each other to pieces. The owner of one of the birds was a huge Negro who wore a diamond pendant in his left ear. The men bet on the cocks with quarters, halves, ones and fives. It was an eerie scene, with about a third of the onlookers spattered with the blood of the birds. The fight we saw lasted about a half hour before one of the cocks dropped dead, torn to pieces. There were four fights in all.

A "coal-dealer's" house of prostitution in Brooklyn, a big unpainted barn reached through a dark, foul alley. A "coal-dealer" is a white man with a string of colored girls. The patronage of the house was strictly white, the prices high, the gals exotic and young. "We get the best people," the proprietor told us, "men who are looking for a different kind of kick."

A traveling crap game with three portable dice tables going and colored pros rolling for the house. The room was jammed, with every table crowded, and the money on the boards was pretty big. Patronage was mixed colored and white; there's no segregation in the underworld. Taxi drivers were "steerers" for the game.

Dawn was breaking when the Olds pulled up in front of the Mecklenburg. "Hope you got your story," said Charlie. "But I'll say it again—I like this town. In spite of what you've seen, it's better than most."

I hung around Charlotte for a few days more, enjoying the excellent French cuisine at the Mecklenburg and quietly digging a little information on my own.

APPENDIX

One of the things I learned was that Charlotte has a serious off-beat sex problem. The Director of the Charlotte Youth Bureau, Detective Neal Forney, recently broke up a sex perversion ring involving a blackmail racket which had preyed on businessmen. Thirty-one men and boys were arrested and brought to trial in Mecklenburg County Superior Court on charges of committing "crimes against nature." Fifteen of those arrested were high school students, and they represented all but one of Charlotte's high schools, which shows that the perversion problem is pretty widespread. The case broke when Forney and his men arrested a 16-year-old youth and a man in a midtown parking lot about a week before I got to Charlotte. The youths would "proposition" older men, and then have pictures taken with a hidden camera. The pictures would then be used to blackmail the victims. All but one of those arrested were white. One "man" arrested in the round-up wore a yellow sun-back dress, high-heeled shoes, and feminine undergarments; he had on lipstick, fingernail polish and rouge, and wore his hair shoulder-length. He was "married" to a traveling salesman! You don't expect such stuff in a small city like Charlotte, but there it was. (Of those arrested, fifteen pleaded guilty and the rest nolo contendere—no defense.)

Where there is a homo problem there is usually a dope problem, and that's true of this Paris of the Piedmont. Shortly before I got to town, two Baltimore agents of the Treasury Department's Narcotic Bureau, cooperating with the North Carolina Bureau of Investigation, smashed a $1,000,000-a-year drug ring operating between Baltimore and Charlotte. The Baltimore agents came down to North Carolina, got into the ring by pretending to be junkies, and worked in it for six months before pulling the rug out from under the dope smugglers. They nabbed the head of the ring in Reidsville, North Carolina, with $25,000 worth of heroin on him. Charlotte junkies who want to "do up" now have to scrabble for their stuff.

Oddly enough, Charlotte has a bootleg problem. The state of North Carolina is never more than one jump ahead of state-wide Prohibition; liquor is sold through state ABC (Alcoholic Beverage Control) stores and it's illegal to buy it by the drink or oven to display bottles of beer and wine in restaurants. Because people resent paying high hootch taxes, moonshiners do a flourishing business. Recently Mecklenburg County police ABC agents destroyed a big still in the woods just off U.S. Route 29 between Hunter Road and Mineral Springs, only seven miles from downtown Charlotte. The still was heated with green hickory wood, which burns without smoke. It was capable of turning out 40 gallons of raw liquor per run. Over 750 gallons of homemade corn was seized in a haystack in nearby North Iredell. Probably more illegal than legal booze is sold in North Carolina, much to the chagrin of the Charlotte Public Library, which has a unique arrangement with the ABC through which the library gets five percent of the profits of the local legal liquor stores!

Charlotte prides itself on being the cultural capital of the South, but, as a native son pointed out in a magazine article some time ago, the pride is a bit premature. This kill-joy observed that when a certain girly-show put on a midnight performance in one of the town's auditoriums, 1,300 people (mostly men) paid a dollar a piece to see the "Parade of Peaches." This was more dough than the Charlotte Symphony Orchestra had netted in three years. The guy left town shortly after the article appeared.

Charlotte is a pretty hot town, but nobody can accuse the police of nonfeasance. The administration does a good job. The town is the way the people want it, no worse and probably somewhat better than many other cities. A lot of its problems are caused by growing pains—it's one of the fastest-growing cities in the entire country.

But a look beneath the pious, placid surface of this Southern boom town will show you plenty to justify the title "Paris of the Piedmont." The wool-hat peanut pickers from the piney woods of both Carolinas get their money's worth in sin and sex when they hit Charlotte on a Saturday night.

REFERENCES

"Belk, Inc." www.referenceforbusiness.com/history/Al-Be/Belk-Inc.html. Accessed May 17, 2006.

Blythe, LeGette, and Charles Brockman. *Hornet's Nest: The Story of Charlotte and Mecklenburg County.* Charlotte: Public Library of Charlotte and Mecklenburg County, 1961.

Brose, Barbara H. "Discovering Charles Wilkes." HNSA 2004 Conference Papers. www.hnsa.org/conf2004/papers/bbrose.htm. Accessed June 9, 2006.

Charlotte Chamber of Commerce, Historical Timeline. www.charlottechamber.com. Accessed April 15, 2006.

Charlotte Observer, "Famous Charlotte Crimes," October 10, 1959.

"CNN *Larry King Live* Interview With Jessica Hahn, July 14, 2005." transcripts.cnn.com/TRANSCRIPTS/0507/14/lkl.01.html. Accessed June 1, 2006.

Diamant, Jeff. *Heist! The $17 million Loomis Fargo Theft.* Winston-Salem: John F. Blair Press, 2002.

Editorial. "A Glad Welcome." *Harper's Weekly*, May 13, 1871.

Federal Bureau of Investigation Transcript of Rae Carruth Interview, December 17, 1999. news.findlaw.com/legalnews/documents/archive_c. html. Accessed April 30, 2006.

Geringer, Joseph. "Henry Louis Wallace: A Calamity Waiting to Happen." Courtoom Television Newtwork. www.crimelibrary.com/serial_killers/ predators/wallace/preface_1.html. Accessed April 27, 2006.

Graham, W.A. *General Joseph Graham and His Papers On North Carolina Revolutionary History.* Raleigh: Edwards & Broughton, 1904.

Handsel, Joyce. "Early 1800s Gold Mining." The Brevard Station Museum. http://www.brevardstation.com/1800b.html. Accessed April 22, 2006.

Higgins, Tom, and Steve Waid. *Junior Johnson: Brave in Life.* Phoenix: David Bull, 1999.

Knapp, Dr. Richard F. *Golden Promise in the Piedmont: The Story of John Reed's Mine.* Raleigh: North Carolina Office of Archives & History, revised edition, 1999.

Kuralt, Charles. "'Oldest Profession' is no Gold Mine in Charlotte." *Charles Kuralt's People.* www.charleskuraltspeople.com/othernewsarticles/prosti- tutes.html. Accessed June 3, 2006.

Maury, Mary Cash. "The Suicide of W.J. Cash." *The Red Clay Reader* 4 (1967): 8–13.

Mill News. The Great Southern Weekly for Textile Workers. Devoted to the Textile Industries 12, no. 16. Charlotte, October 14, 1920. Property of the North Carolina Collection, University of North Carolina at Chapel Hill.

Mint Museum of Art. "NC Solid Gold Facts." www.mintmuseum.org/ craftingnc/02-02-001-a.htm. Accessed April 22, 2006.

Morrill, Dr. Dan L. "The Civil Rights Revolution in Mecklenburg County." Charlotte-Mecklenburg Historic Preservation Foundation. www.cmhpf. org/educationcivilrights.htm. Accessed June 14, 2006.

REFERENCES

———. *Historic Charlotte: An Illustrated History of Charlotte and Mecklenburg County*. Historical Pub Network, 2002.

Official Tammy Faye Website. www.tammyfaye.com. Accessed May 31, 2006.

Reed Gold Mine. www.ah.dcr.state.nc.us/Sections/hs/reed/reed.htm. Accessed April 22, 2006.

Sharp, Frankie. "Chicago Gang Lifted Over $120,000 From Mail Truck." *Charlotte Observer*, November 11, 1957.

Singer, Mark P., and Ryan L. Sumner. *Auto Racing in Charlotte and the Carolina Piedmont*. Charleston: Arcadia, 2003.

St. George, Donna. "Mending shattered Childhoods: Newborns, Siblings and Substitute Caregivers Endure Reminders of Loss." *Washington Post*, December 21, 2004.

Thomas, Mike. "'Road' well traveled by gangsters." *Illinois Police and Sheriff's News*, July 12, 2002. www.ipsn.org/irish_mobsters.htm. Accessed May 19, 2006.

Time, "Back to the Roaring '20s," October 19, 1942. time-proxy.yaga.com/time/archive/preview/0,10987,850055,00.html. Accessed May 19, 2006.

Tuohy, John William. "The Owl." *Gambling Magazine*. www.gamblingmagazine.com/articles/53/53-95.htm. Accessed May 19, 2006.

Wacker, Grant. "Jim Bakker and the Eternal Revenue Service." *Christian Century*, November 15, 1989.

Web Resources for NC Educators. "Facts about the Reed Gold Mine."www.itpi.dpi.state.nc.us/reed/reed/facts/facts2.html. Accessed April 22, 2006.

Weiss, Bill, and Marshall Wright. "Team #56 The Charlotte Hornets." www.minorleaguebaseball.com. Accessed June 25, 2006.

York, John. "Commando-Like Gang Makes Big Haul at Belk's." *Charlotte Observer*, April 3, 1967.